HELVETIA
souvenir

*Die Schönheit der Schweiz, vor-
gestellt in 180 Farbfotos.*

*Les beautés de la Suisse, présen-
tées en 180 photos-couleurs.*

*The beauty of Switzerland in 180 co-
lor photographs.*

*Le bellezze della Svizzera presentate
in 180 fotografie a colori.*

*La bellezza de Suiza, presentada en
180 fotos en color.*

HELVETIA
souvenir

Verlag-Edition
PHOTOGLOB AG, Zürich
Text & Design
DINO SASSI

Willkommen in der Schweiz! In diesem kleinen Land von kaum mehr als 40.000 Quadratkilometern im Herzen Europas erwartet Sie eine solche Vielfalt von Landschafts- und Lebensformen, wie in keinem anderen Land vergleichbarer Grösse. Hier eröffnet sich Ihnen die Alpenwelt in ihrem ganzen Zauber; mit ihren gewaltigen und majestätischen Gipfeln, den kristallklaren Bergseen und ausgedehnten Wäldern. Friedliche grüne Weiden wechseln ab mit intensiv genutzten Feldern. Gepflegte Weinberge überziehen die sanften Hänge um den Genfersee, während das malerische Tessin mit seinem milden Klima bereits die Nähe des Mittelmeeres ahnen lässt. Berge bedecken den grössten Teil der Landesfläche und prägen den Charakter der Schweiz in entscheidendem Masse. Im Gebirge findet man den grössten Reichtum an landschaftlicher Schönheit, die wichtigsten Zentren des Fremdenverkehrs und die bevorzugten Erholunsgebiete. Die alten Traditionen und volkstümlichen Bräuche, die immer noch voll Kraft und Leben sind, üben auf den Besucher einen starken Reiz aus. Ueberall zeugen Burgen, Schlösser und Herrensitze, Kathedralen und Kunstdenkmäler von der reichen kulturhistorischen Vergangenheit des Landes. Die Schweiz hat nicht nur eine fesselnde Vergangenheit, sie ist auch ein modernes Land von grösstem Interesse. Sie ist nämlich ein einmaliges Beispiel für das Zusammenleben verschiedener Kulturen, Religionen, Traditionen und Sprachen – Deutsch, Französisch, Italienisch und Rätoromanisch sind die offiziellen Landessprachen - in einer Nation. Statt die Integration zu erschweren, erweist sich diese Verschiedenartigkeit als Quelle gegenseitiger Bereicherung und scheint die harmonische Entwicklung der Gesellschaft anzuregen. Die politischen Institutionen sind von einem Geiste absoluter Freiheit und Eigenständigkeit geprägt und gewährleisten dem Bürger Formen der direkten oder indirekten Demokratie, wie sie nur wenige Staaten zu bieten haben. Es ist die sogenannte Schweizer Zivilisation, eine erstaunliche gesellschaftspolitische Alchimie, fast ein Symbol, ein Modell, das sich die Völker unserer Zeit immer häufiger zum Leitbild nehmen. Dieses bescheidene Werk kann und will nicht den Anspruch erheben, die Schweiz erschöpfend darzustellen. Es möchte den Leser vielmehr auf sympathische Weise an seinen Besuch erinnern. Wir sind überzeugt, dass ihm das eine oder andere Bild eine romantische Seefahrt, eine belebende Wanderung in der frischen Alpenluft oder die stimmungsvolle Atmosphäre einer mittelalterlichen Burg ins Gedächtnis rufen wird. Andere Bilder von Orten, die er nie gesehen hat, werden in ihm vielleicht den Wunsch wecken, dieses kleine und doch grosse Land besser kennenzulernen.

Bienvenue en Suisse! Ce petit pays (à peine plus de 40.000 kilomètres carrés), situé au cœur de l'Europe, vous offre une variété incomparable de paysages et de modes de vie, réunie nulle part ailleurs au monde sur une surface si réduite. Vous pénétrez ici dans l'enchantement de l'univers alpestre, avec ses sommets majestueux, ses lacs de montagne cristallins et ses vastes forêts. Les prairies vertes et paisibles alternent avec les champs de culture intensive. Des vignobles soignés s'étendent sur les coteaux du lac Léman, tandis que le Tessin pittoresque, au climat doux, laisse pressentir le voisinage de la Méditerranée. Les montagnes occupent la plus grande partie du pays et déterminent de manière décisive le caractère de la Suisse. On y trouve les paysages les plus prestigieux, les principaux centres touristiques et les lieux de séjour favoris. Les anciennes traditions et les coutumes populaires, restées vivaces, exercent une grande fascination sur le visiteur. En tous lieux, on rencontre forteresses, châteaux et manoirs, cathédrales et monuments architecturaux, témoins d'un riche passé historique et culturel. Si le passé de la Suisse est captivant, le pays moderne présente, lui aussi, un grand intérêt. Des régions de culture, religion et tradition différente coexistent dans une même nation, et l'on compte quatre langues officielles: l'allemand, le français, l'italien et le romanche. Un tel exemple est unique. Au lieu de créer des difficultés d'intégration, cette diversité est bien plutôt source d'enrichissement réciproque et semble stimuler un développement harmonieux de la société. Les institutions politiques sont empreintes d'un esprit d'entière liberté et d'indépendance, et elles offrent au citoyen des formes de démocratie directe et indirecte connues dans peu d'Etats seulement. Il s'agit de la "civilisation suisse", une alchimie politico-sociale surprenante, pour ainsi dire un symbole, un modèle dont les nations actuelles s'inspirent toujours plus fréquemment. Ce modeste ouvrage ne saurait prétendre à une description complète de la Suisse. Il voudrait bien plutôt offrir au lecteur un rappel agréable de sa visite. Nous sommes certains que, au gré des images, il se remémorera une croisière romantique, une promenade stimulante dans l'air frais des Alpes ou l'atmosphère d'un fort moyenâgeux. Quant aux vues de lieux qu'il n'a pas visités, elles l'inciteront peut-être à découvrir encore mieux ce petit pays pourtant si grand.

Welcome to Switzerland! In this small country of scarcely more than 40,000 square kilometres at the very heart of Europe you can look forward to seeing a variety of landscapes and ways of life not to be found in any other country of comparable size. Here, all the magic of the Alpine world is open to you with its huge and majestic peaks, crystal-clear mountain lakes and extensive forests. Peaceful green meadows alternate with intensively cultivated fields. Well-tended vineyards cover the gentle slopes around the Lake of Geneva while, in the picturesque Tessin with its mild climate, one has the impression of being in the vicinity of the Mediterranean. Most of Switzerland is covered by mountains and these have had a decisive influence on its character. In the mountains are to be found the most fabulous scenery, the most important foreign touristcentres and favourite holidays areas. The old traditions and folklore, which are still strongly maintained, are a great attraction for visitors. The citadels, castles and manors, cathedrals and monuments which abound provide evidence of the rich cultural and historical past of the country. Switzerland does not just have a fascinating past; it is also a modern country of the greatest interest. It is, in fact, a unique example of different cultures, religions, traditions and languages – German, French, Italian and Rhaeto-Romansch being the official languages of the country – living together as one nation. Instead of making integration more difficult, this diversity has turned out to be the source of mutual enrichment and seems to stimulate the harmonious evolution of the community. The political institutions are characterized by a spirit of absolute freedom and independence and they guarantee the citizen forms of direct or indirect democracy such as few states have to offer. This is the so-called Swiss Civilization, an astonishing sociopolitical alchemy, almost a symbol, a model that the people of our time are more and more frequently taking as an example. This modest work cannot and does not claim to describe Switzerland in an exhaustive manner. It aims, rather, to provide readers with a pleasant reminder of their visit. We feel certain that one or other of the pictures will call to mind a romantic trip on a lake, an invigorating walk in the fresh Alpine air or the impressive atmosphere of a medieval castle. Other pictures of places that the reader has not yet seen may perhaps create a desire to become better acquainted with this small yet great country.

envenuti in Svizzera! In questo piccolo
aese di poco più di 40.000 chilometri
uadrati, nel cuore dell'Europa, troverete
na tale varietà di paesaggi e realtà uma-
e come non è dato di riscontrare in
essun altro paese di uguale superficie.
ui vi attendono il mondo magico della
ontagna con le Alpi maestose ed impo-
enti; i laghi di cristallo, le grandi foreste
perdita d'occhio. Verdi e tranquilli pa-
coli si alternano a colture intensive; se-
ionati vigneti ricoprono le dolci colline
el Lago Lemano, mentre il pittoresco
icino ci ricorda, con il suo mite clima,
he non siamo lontani dal Mediterraneo.
a montagna occupa la gran parte del
erritorio, e naturalmente ciò caratterizza
ortemente la Svizzera. Alla montagna
ono quindi connesse le maggiori varietà
i paesaggio, di attività turistiche e ri-
reative. Le antiche tradizioni ed il folklo-
e, ancora forti e vitali, sono motivo di
rande interesse per i visitatori.
castelli, le fortezze, le residenze regali,
e cattedrali, gli innumerevoli monumenti
parsi su tutto il territorio testimoniano il
cco passato storico-culturale del pae-
e. Ma oltre che per questo suo affasci-
ante passato, la Svizzera è estrema-
ente interessante come Paese moder-
o. Essa rappresenta infatti un caso uni-
o di nazione in cui convivono culture,
eligioni, tradizioni, lingue diverse – quat-
ro sono le lingue principali, tedesco-
rancese-italiano-ladino – le quali, invece
i ostacolare l'integrazione, sembrano
rricchirsi le une con le altre e favorire
armonico sviluppo della società. Le isti-
uzioni politiche, improntate ad uno spiri-
o di assoluta libertà ed autonomia, ga-
antiscono al cittadino forme di democra-
ia diretta od indiretta come pochi paesi
ossono offrire ai loro popoli. È la cosid-
etta civiltà svizzera, meravigliosa alchi-
ia socio-politica divenuta quasi un sim-
olo e un modello al quale fanno sem-
re più volentieri riferimento le società
oderne.
Questo semplice volume non può e non
uole trattare compiutamente la Svizzera,
na si prefigge di fornire al lettore un
impatico ricordo della sua visita. Siamo
icuri che molte di queste immagini lo
iporteranno ad una romantica gita sul
ago, ad una rivitalizzante escursione nel-
aria fina delle Alpi, all'atmosfera sugge-
tiva di un castello medievale. Altre im-
agini di luoghi non visitati lo indurranno,
orse, a ritornare ed a voler conoscere
iù a fondo questo piccolo, grande pae-
e.

¡Bienvenido a Suiza! En este país situado
en pleno centro de Europa, cuya superficie apenas supera los 40.000 kilómetros
cuadrados, le espera una variedad de
paisajes y de formas de vida que no
podrá encontrar en ningún otro país de
tamaño comparable. Aquí podrá admirar
el mundo de los Alpes, en todo su
esplendor y encanto, con sus imponentes y majestuosas cumbres, lagos de
montaña con agua cristalina y bosques
de gran extensión. Pacíficos pastos
verdes. Viñedos cuidados con el máximo
esmero cubren las suaves colinas situa-
das alrededor del lago de Ginebra, mien-
tras que el pintoresco Tesino, con su
suave clima, permite presentir la proximi-
dad del Mediterráneo. Las montañas
cubren la mayor parte de la superficie
del país, y marcan de manera inequívoca
el carácter de Suiza. La mayor riqueza de
belleza rural, los más importantes centros
del turismo extranjero y los centros
predilectos de vacaciones se encuentran en la región montañosa. Las antiguas tradiciones y las costumbres populares, que todavía conservan su pleno
esplendor y vida, constituyen un intenso
y agradable atractivo para el visitante. las
fortalezas, los castillos y las viviendas
residenciales, así como las catedrales y
los monumentos de arte atestiguan en
todas partes el rico pasado histórico-
cultural del país. Ahora bien, Suiza no
sólo cuenta con un pasado fascinante,
sino que es igualmente un moderno país
del máximo interés. Se trata de un
ejemplo sin igual de convivencia de
diferentes culturas, religiones, tradiciones e idiomas -los idiomas oficiales del
país son el alemán, el francés, el italiano
y el romanche- concentrados en una
nación. En lugar de dificultar la integra-
ción, esta heterogeneidad se manifiesta
como una fuente de enriquecimiento
común, y estimula, según parece, el
desarrollo armonioso de la sociedad. Las
instituciones políticas se caracterizan
por un espíritu de libertad y autonomía
absolutos, y aseguran al ciudadano formas de democracia directa o indirecta
como las que sólo muy pocos Estados
pueden ofrecer. Se trata de la así llamada
civilización suiza, una asombrosa alqui-
mia sociopolítica, casi un símbolo, un
modelo, que los diferentes pueblos de
nuestro tiempo van tomando, cada vez
más, como imagen diretriz. Esta modesta
obra no puede ni desea pretender pre-
sentar Suiza en forma exhaustiva. Lo que
desea es recordar más bien al lector su
visita en forma simpática. Estamos con-
vencidos de que una u otra imagen
despertarán interesantes recuerdos de
un romántico viaje en un lago, una inte-
resante excursión respirando el aire
fresco de los Alpes o el impresionante
ambiente de una fortaleza de la Edad
Media. Es muy posible que otras imáge-
nes de lugares que nunca vio despierten
en él el deseo de conocer mejor este
pequeño "gran" país.

スイスへようこそ！　ヨーロッパの心臓部に位置するスイスは国土面積
40,000km²たらずの小国です。しかし、他のどんな国とも比較しがたい変
化に富んだ自然と多様な人々の暮らしがそこにはあります。万
年雪に覆われた壮厳なアルプスの峰々、清冽な水をたたえた山間の湖そし
て遙かに広がる美しい森林など、あらゆる魅力を備えたアルプスの世界
が展開するのがスイスなのです。のどかに広がる緑の草原を縫って、整
然と耕された畑が点在、そして手入れの行き届いたぶどう畑がレマン湖
の辺りのなだらかな丘陵地帯に続いています。絵のように美しいテッシ
ン州のおだやかな気候は既に地中海の香りをただよわせています。

スイスの特長は何んといっても険しい山岳地帯が国土の大半を覆ってい
ること。この結果、厳しい迄に美しい山岳美や深い峡谷といった変化の
ある景観がいたるところで楽しめます。観光の中心地となる町々や保養
地はそれぞれ独特の雰囲気とたたずまいを見せて、人々を魅了せずには
おきません。そしてスイスの人々が大切にしている古い伝統や風俗は今
も脈々と生き続けているのです。美しく気高いアルプスの峰々を仰ぎ、
点在する古い城や館そして教会、過去の歴史を残す記念碑の数々などは、
まさしくスイスの豊かな歴史的な過去と芸術的な遺産を見事に証明して
います。

ハプスブルグ家の支配に抗して立ち上がった3つのカントン、ウリ、シ
ュヴィーツ、ウンターヴァルデン、そして13世紀の戦いで大きな役割を
果たしたウンターヴァルデンの伝説的な英雄、ウィリアム・テルは自由の
闘士として、その名を知らない人はいないでしょう。このドラマティッ
クな出来事がスイス連邦を創設する発端となり、その後、更に今日のス
イスを構成している他のカントンや自治体が連邦に参加をしたのでした。

しかしながら、スイスはこうした歴史的な過去のロマンだけを持ってい
るわけではありません。それと同時に極めて興味深い近代国家でもある
わけです。つまり、さまざまなスイスの文化、宗教、伝統や風俗そして
多数の言語が共存している国家なのです。ドイツ語、フランス語、イタ
リア語そしてロマンシュ語が単一の国家であるスイスの公用語となって
います。この多様性は統合を困難にするどころか、お互いを豊かにする
源泉であり、また社会の調和的発展の原動力であると思われます。政治
的制度は絶対的な自由と独立の精神を基本にしていて、ほんのひと握り
の国家しか実現させていない、直接および間接の民主主義を、スイスで
は市民に保証しています。これがいわゆるスイスの文化であり、いわば、
驚くべき社会的政治的な錬金術ともいえるものであり、現代の諸国民が
指導理念として、切に希求しているひとつのシンボルともモデルともい
えるものなのです。

このささやかな作品はスイスを余すところなく描きだそうとは思ってお
りませんし、またそれを意図としているわけではありません。そのささ
やかな目的は、読者がかつてスイスを訪れた、その思い出を想起して頂
こうとしているのに外なりません。わたくし達はこの写真、あるいはそ
の写真をご覧になって、ロマンティックな湖の旅、新鮮な空気の中を爽
快な気分で山歩きをしたこと…、そして詩情豊かな古城の面影を読者の
心の中に再び呼びさますことを願っております。また読者の皆さまが、
まだ訪れたことないスイス各地の写真をご覧になる時、多分読者の心の
内に、小国ではあるけれど大きな豊かな国スイスをもっとお知りになり
たいという望みをいだくことでしょう。

Beidseits des Rheinknies, am Dreiländereck Schweiz-Deutschland-Frankreich, liegt **Basel,** ein Industriezentrum ersten Ranges mit grossen chemischen Konzernen. Bedeutende Kunstdenkmäler zeugen von seiner stolzen Vergangenheit.

Bâle est située sur un coude du Rhin et s'étend de part et d'autre du fleuve, au point de rencontre des trois pays: Suisse, Allemagne et France. Avec la présence de grands trusts de chimie, elle est un centre industriel de première importance. Des monuments artistiques remarquables témoignent de son passé brillant.

Basle is located astride the Rhine where Switzerland, Germany and France meet. It is a leading industrial centre and the home of several huge chemical complexes. Many monuments bear witness to its glorious past.

Situata a cavallo di una grande ansa del Reno, al confine con Francia e Germania, **Basilea** è oggi un primario centro industriale, soprattutto chimico. Essa conserva imponenti monumenti a testimonianza del suo antico passato.

La ciudad de **Basilea** se encuentra a ambos lados del codo que forma el Rin en el lugar donde se tocan los tres paises Suiza-Alemania-Francia. Es un centro industrial de primer order donde se encuentran grandes Grupos de empresas quimicas. Importantes monumentos artisticos dan clara prueba de su orgulloso pasado.

Am Marktplatz steht das reich verzierte, mit Fassadenmalereien geschmückte Rathaus aus dem 16. Jh.

A la place du Marché se trouve l'Hôtel de ville du XVIᵉ siècle, aux façades richement ornées de peintures.

Down one side of the Market Place is the richly decorated facade of the 16th century Town Hall.

Sulla Marktplatz si erge imponente il palazzo Comunale, costruito nel XVI secolo con decorazioni ed affreschi murali. A destra la porta dell'antica cerchia muraria detta «Spalentor».

En la «Marktplatz» (Plaza del Mercado) se encuentra el Ayuntamiento del siglo XVI, ricamente adornado con pinturas en las fachadas.

Der Rheinhafen ist der Zugang zur einzigen Wasserstrasse, die die Schweiz mit dem Meer verbindet. Ein grosser Teil der für den Export bestimmten Schweizer Waren werden hier verschifft.

Le port du Rhin donne accès à la seule voie fluviale reliant la Suisse à la mer. Une grande partie de la production suisse destinée à l'exportation y est embarquée.

The Rhine Port is the gateway to the only waterway connection that Switzerland has with the sea. Many Swiss export goods are shipped from here.

Il porto sul Reno è l'unica via d'acqua che congiunge la Svizzera al mare e dal quale parte la metà di tutte le merci svizzere destinate all'esportazione.

El puerto del Rin permite el acceso a la única vía acuática que enlaza Suiza con el mar. Una gran parte de las mercancías suizas destinadas a la exportación se embarcan en este lugar.

Spalentor

Rheinfelden

Laufenburg

Zurzach

▶

Baden im Kanton Aargau liegt am Ufer der Limmat. Sehenswert das Landvogteischloss aus dem 15. Jh. Seine Thermalquellen waren bereits zur Römerzeit geschätzt und werden auch jetzt noch rege genutzt.

Baden est située dans le canton d'Argovie, sur les rives de la Limmat. Il vaut la peine de visiter le château des baillis du XVᵉ siècle. Les sources thermales, appréciées au temps des Romains déjà, sont abondamment utilisées aujourd'hui encore.

Baden in the canton of Aargau, lies on the banks of the Limmat. The 15th century castle of the local governor is worth a visit. The health spas were much appreciated back in Roman times and are still very much in use today.

Baden, nel Cantone di Argovia, è situata sul fiume Limmat. Caratteristico il castello del Balivo del XIV sec. Le sue acque termali erano già conosciute dai Romani e sfruttate anche nel Medioevo. Oggi è sede di industrie molto diversificate.

Baden, ciudad del Cantón de Argovia, se encuentra a orillas del río Limmat. Es digno de ver el castillo, con el calabozo del pais, del siglo XIII. Sus fuentes termales eran ya apreciadas en la época de los romanos, y siguen teniendo igualmente gran aceptación en la actualidad.

Aarau am Ufer der Aare ist die Hauptstadt des Kantons Aargau.

Aarau, sur le rives de l'Aar, est le chef-lieu du canton d'Argovie.

Aarau is the capital of Canton Aargau and it lies on the banks of the Aare.

Aarau, sul fiume Aare, è il capoluogo del Cantone di Argovia.

Aarau, a orillas del río Aar, es la capital del cantón de Argovia.

Zofingen

Liestal ist die Hauptstadt des Halbkantons Basel-Land.

Liestal est le chef-lieu du demi-canton de Bâle-Campagne.

Liestal is the capital of the semi-canton of Basle Rural.
▼

Liestal è il capoluogo del semi-Cantone di Basilea-Campagna.

Liestal es la capital del semicantón Basilea-Campaña.

Olten an der Aare ist ein bedeutendes Industriezentrum des Kantons Solothurn und gleichzeitig ein wichtiger Knotenpunkt des Strassen– und Schienenverkehrs.

Olten, centre industriel d'envergure situé sur l'Aar, dans le canton de Soleure, est également un nœud routier et ferroviaire important.

Olten on the Aare is an important industrial centre in the canton of Solothurn as well as being an important road and railway junction.

Olten, sul fiume Aare, è un importante centro industriale del Cantone di Soletta. È anche un attivo nodo stradale e ferroviario.

Olten, a orillas del Aar, es el centro industrial más importante del cantón Solothurn y, al mismo tiempo, un importante nudo del tráfico rodado y ferroviario.

Zürich, Hauptstadt des gleichnamigen Kantons, ist zugleich die grösste Stadt der Schweiz und das bedeutendste wirtschaftliche, industrielle und kulturelle Zentrum des Landes. Es ist am nördlichen Ende des Zürichsees gelegen, am Zusammenfluss der Limmat und der Sihl. In Richtung Süden bietet sich ein grossartiger Ausblick über den See auf die majestätische Alpenkette.

Zurich, chef-lieu du canton de même nom, est la plus grande ville de Suisse et, en même temps, son centre économique, industriel et culturel le plus important. Elle est située à l'extrémité nord du lac de Zurich, au confluent de la Limmat et de la Sihl. Vers le sud, une vue splendide s'étend sur le lac et la majestueuse chaîne des Alpes.

Zurich is the capital of the canton of the same name, it is also the biggest town in Switzerland and the main economic, industrial and cultural centre in the country. It lies on the northern tip of lake Zurich, where the rivers Limmat and Sihl converge. To the south, there is a splendid view of the majestic Alpine chain across the Lake.

Capoluogo dell'omonimo cantone, *Zurigo* è anche la più grande città della Svizzera, il maggior centro economico, industriale e culturale di tutto il Paese. È situata sulla sponda settentrionale del lago di Zurigo, alla confluenza dei due fiumi Limmat e Sihl ed il suo orizzonte meridionale è chiuso dalla maestosa visione delle Alpi.

Zurich capital del cantón del mismo nombre, es al mismo tiempo la más grande ciudad de Suiza y la más importante desde los puntos de vista económico, industrial y cultural del país. Está situada en el extremo norte del lago de Zurich, en la confluencia de los rios Limmat y Sihl. Hacia el sur se ofrece una vista imponente, sobre el lago, hacia la majestuosa cadena de los Alpes.

Der Hauptbahnhof mit der weltberühmten Bahnhofstrasse ist einer der beliebtesten und belebtesten Treffpunkte der Stadt.

La gare principale et la Bahnhofstrasse mondialement connue comptent parmi les points de rencontre particulièrement appréciés pour leur animation.

The Main Railway Station and the world famous Station Road – Bahnhofstrasse – is one of the favourite and liveliest meeting points of the town.

La Stazione centrale (Hauptbahnhof) è uno dei punti d'incontro preferiti e più affollati della città.

La estación ferroviaria principal, con la mundialmente conocida «Bahnhofstrasse» (Calle de la Estación) es uno de los puntos de reunión más estimados y animados de la ciudad.

Das Schweizerische Landesmuseum beherbergt Werke der Malerei, Bildhauerei und der Handwerkskunst aus verschiedenen Epochen, von der Steinzeit bis 1800.

Le Musée national suisse abrite des œuvres de peinture, de sculpture et d'artisanat jusqu'en 1800.

The Swiss National Museum houses paintings, carvings and handicrafts of various periods from the Stone Age up to 1800.

Il Museo nazionale Svizzero raccoglie opere di pittura, scultura ed artigianato di diverse epoche, dalla preistoria fino al 1800.

El Museo Nacional suizo contiene obras de pintura, escultura y artesanía de diferentes épocas, desde la Edad de la Piedra, hasta 1800.

Das Grossmünster mit seinen markanten Zwillingstürmen, dessen Entstehung in die karolingische Zeit fällt, ist das bedeutendste mittelalterliche Bauwerk der Stadt.

Le Grossmünster, dont l'origine remonte à l'époque carolingienne, est, avec ses tours jumelles typiques, l'édifice moyenâgeux le plus important de la ville.

The Great Minster, with its eye-catching twin towers, going back to the Carolingian era, is the main building surviving from the Middle Ages.

La Collegiata (Grossmunster) dalle due superbe torri, è il più importante monumento medievale di Zurigo, fondata in età carolingia.

«Grossmünster», con sus llamativas torres gemelas, construida en la época de los carolingios, es la obra más importante de la Edad Media de la ciudad.

Im Herzen Zürichs drängt sich, auf beiden Seiten der Limmat, die Altstadt mit ihrer herzlichen und gastfreundlichen Atmosphäre. Im Wasser des Flusses spiegeln sich das Stadthaus, das Fraumünster und die St. Peters Kirche.

Au cœur de Zurich, la vieille ville à l'atmosphère chaleureuse et accueillante est implantée, dense, sur les deux rives de la Limmat. L'Hôtel de ville, le Fraumünster et l'église St-Pierre se reflètent dans les eaux de la rivière.

The heart of Zurich, clustered on each bank of the Limmat, is the Old Town with its warm and friendly atmosphere. The waters of the river reflect the Town Hall, the Fraumünster and St. Peter's Church.

Nel cuore della metropoli, raccolta sulle sponde del Limmat, si trova la città vecchia, con la sua atmosfera cordiale ed accogliente. Sulle acque del fiume si riflettono la Stadthaus, il Fraumünster, e la Peterskirche.

A ambos lados del rio Limmat, en pleno corazón de Zurich, se encuentra la parte antigua de la ciudad con su ambiente cordial y hospitalario. En el agua del rio se reflejan el edificio del Ayuntamiento, la catedral Fraumünster y la iglesia St. Peter.

Im alten Stadtkern erinnern die engen, verschlungenen
Gässchen und die schlanken Kirchtürme an Zürichs grosse
und faszinierende Vergangenheit. Auf den sanft abfallenden
Hügeln rings um die Stadt erstrecken sich die neuen, moder-
nen Wohnquartiere.

Dans le noyau ancien de la ville, les ruelles tortueuses et les
clochers élancés rappellent le passé riche et fascinant de
Zurich. Les quartiers d'habitation modernes s'étendent sur les
collines en pente douce qui environnent la ville.

The narrow, winding alleys and the slender church steeples of
the heart of the Old town are reminiscent of Zurich's great and
fascinating past. The gently undulating hills around the Town
are dotted with new, modern residential developments.

Nell'antico centro di Zurigo, le stradine strette e tortuose, i
campanili alti e svettanti, ricordano le ricche ed affascinanti
vicende storiche della città. Tutt'intorno, sulle colline degra-
danti, sorgono i nuovi e moderni quartieri residenziali.

Las estrechas callejuelas y esbeltas torres de las iglesias del
núcleo antiguo de la ciudad recuerdan el fascinante pasado
de Zurich. En las colinas que descienden suavemente en todo
el entorno de la ciudad se extienden los nuevos y modernos
barrios residenciales.

The **Rhine Falls** near Schaffhausen are the biggest and most impressive waterfall in Europe. With a span of 490 feet it sends a churning mass of water hurtling down a rock face of over 60 feet high. This spectacle is observed from Laufen Castle perched on high. The Old Town of **Schaffhausen** lies in the shadow of Munot, an old fortress.

Le **cascate del Reno** a **Sciaffusa** sono le più grandi ed imponenti d'Europa, alte m. 20 e larghe m. 150. Esse sono dominate dall'alto dal Castello di Woerth. Nel centro della città vecchia il forte Munot.

Keltisch-römischer abstammung ist heute **Winterthur** ein grosses Handels- und Industriezentrum.

D'origine cetique-romaine, **Winterthur** est aujourd'hui un grand centre commercial et industriel.

Of romano-celtic origins, **Winterthur** is today an important commercial and industrial centre.

Di origine celtico romana, **Winterthur** è oggi un grande centro commerciale ed industriale.

De origen celta-románico, **Winterthur** hoy es un gran centro comercial y industrial.

Der **Rheinfall** bei Schaffhausen ist der grösste und eindrücklichste Wasserfall Europas. Auf einer Breite von 150 m stürzen die tosenden Wassermassen 20 m in die Tiefe. Von oben bewacht das Schloss Laufen dieses Schauspiel. Die Altstadt von **Schaffhausen** wird vom Munot, einer alten Befestigungsanlage, beherrscht.

Les **chutes du Rhin**, près de Schaffhouse, sont les plus grandes et les plus impressionnantes d'Europe. Sur une largeur de 150 m, les flots tumultueux se précipitent à une profondeur de 20 m. Le château de Laufen, situé au-dessus, semble surveiller le spectacle. La vieille ville de **Schaffhouse** est dominée par le Munot, une ancienne fortification.

El «**Rheinfall**» (Salto del Rin) en **Schaf-hausen** es el salto de agua más grande e impresionante de Europa. Las ruidosas masas de agua se precipitan, en un ancho de 150 m, a 20 m de profundidad. El castillo Laufen vigila desde arriba este maravilloso espectáculo. La parte antigua de la ciudad de **Schaffhausen** está dominada por Munot, una antigua instalación defensiva.

Kreuzlingen liegt an de
Landesgrenze und ist mit dem
auf deutschem Gebiet gelege
nen Konstanz praktisch z
einem einzigen Stadtgebiet zu
sammengewachsen.

Kreuzlingen est située sur la
frontière nationale et forme
pratiquement une seule agglo
mération avec Constance, si
tuée sur territoire allemand.

Kreuzlingen is located or
the national boundary and has
virtually grown to form a single
township with the city o
Konstanz on the German side.

Kreuzlingen è sul confine co
la Germania, praticamente ur
unico centro urbano con la cit
tà di Costanza.

Kreuzlingen se encuentra er
el límite del país, y forma
prácticamente una sola ciudad
con Costanza, situada en terri
torio alemán.

Die Fassadenmalereien in kräftigen
Farben und die blumengeschmückten
Balkone verleihen **Stein am Rhein**
einen ganz besonderen Reiz. Das
heitere, ausgezeichnet erhaltene
Städtchen aus dem Mittelalter liegt an
der Stelle, wo der Rhein auf seinem
Lauf nach Norden den Bodensee wieder verlässt.

Les façades peintes de couleurs vives
et les balcons fleuris confèrent à **Stein
am Rhein** un attrait tout particulier.
Cette riante cité moyenâgeuse, admi-
rablement conservée, est située à l'endroit où le Rhin quitte le lac de Constance pour reprendre son cours vers
le nord.

The brightly painted facades and
flower-bedecked balconies of **Stein-
am-Rhein** give this little town a very
special air. This cheerful, beautifully
preserved little town which dates back
to the Middle Ages is located at the
place where the Rhine leaves Lake
Constance to make its way north.

Le pareti esterne delle case dipinte
con figure a vivaci colori, balconi fioriti,
caratterizzano **Stein am Rhein**, una ridente cittadina medievale, splendida-
mente conservata, che sorge sulla riva
destra del Reno dove questo esce dal
Lago di Costanza.

Las pinturas de las fachadas, en inten-
sos colores, y los balcones adornados
con flores prestan a **Stein am Rhein** un
encanto realmente especial. La alegre
pequeña ciudad de la Edad Media,
conservada maravillosamente, se encuentra en el lugar donde el Rin aban-
dona de nuevo el Bodensee para con-
tinuar su curso hacia el norte.

Scheffel's Weinstube

Romanshorn im Kanton Thurgau ist ein betriebsamer Hafen mit Fährverbindungen von der Schweiz nach Deutschland.

Romanshorn, dans le canton de Thurgovie, possède un port actif, avec bac reliant la Suisse et l'Allemagne.

Romanshorn in the canton of Thurgau is a busy little port from which boats ply to and fro between Switzerland and Germany.

Romanshorn, nel Cantone di Turgovia, è un vivace porto con traffico di navi traghetto ferroviarie tra la Svizzera e la Germania.

Romanshorn, situado en el cantón de Thurgau, es un puerto de gran actividad con enlaces entre Suiza y Alemania.

Rorschach ist ein hübsches Städtchen am Bodensee. Sehenswert sind die alten Patrizierhäuser.

Rorschach est une charmante petite ville située sur les rives du lac de Constance. Les anciennes maisons particiennes valent le coup d'œil.

Rorschach is a pretty little town on Lake Constance. The stately old town houses are worth a visit.

Rorschach è una graziosa cittadina con un attivo porticciuolo turistico. Notevoli sono le antiche case patrizie.

Rorschach es una bella pequeña ciudad situada a orillas del Bodensee. Son dignas de mención las antiguas mansiones de los patricios.

St. Gallen, *die Hauptstadt des gleichnamigen Kantons, liegt zwischen dem Bodensee und dem von der Säntisgruppe beherrschten Alpenmassiv. Die Erzeugnisse der Textilindustrie und die St. Galler Spitzen und Stickereien sind in der ganzen Welt berühmt.*

St-Gall, chef-lieu du canton de même nom, est située entre le lac de Constance et le massif alpin dominé par le Säntis. Les produits de l'industrie textile ainsi que les dentelles et broderies de St-Gall sont réputés dans le monde entier.

St. Gallen, *the capital of the canton of the same name, lies between Lake Constance and the Alpine block crowned by the Säntis peaks. The products of the textile industry and St. Gallen lace and embroidery work are famous throughout the world.*

San Gallo è il capoluogo dell'omonimo Cantone, situata tra il lago di Costanza ed il massiccio delle Alpi, ove domina il gruppo del Saentis. I prodotti tessili, i pizzi ed i ricami di S. Gallo sono conosciuti in tutto il mondo.

San Gall, la capital del cantón del mismo nombre, se encuentra situada entre el Bodensee y el macizo alpino dominado por el grupo Säntis. Los productos de la industria textil, así como los encajes y bordados de San Gall, son famosos en todo el mundo.

Die Kathedrale, ein eindrückliches Beispiel barocker Baukunst, erhebt sich auf den Fundamenten einer früheren Klosterkirche aus der karolingischen Zeit. Die anliegende Stiftsbibliothek enthält eine Vielzahl kostbarer Handschriften aus dem Mittelalter.

La cathédrale, monument marquant de l'architecture baroque, s'élève sur les fondations d'une ancienne église conventuelle de la période carolingienne. La bibliothèque annexée contient un grand nombre de précieux manuscrits du moyen âge.

The Cathedral, an impressive example of Baroque architecture, rises on the foundations of an even earlier cloister church of the Carolingian era. The adjacent monastic library contains a large number of valuable manuscripts dating back to the Middle Ages.

La Cattedrale è un imponente edificio in stile barocco che sorge sulle fondamenta di una precedente chiesa abbaziale carolingia. La biblioteca annessa è ricca di preziosissimi codici medievali.

La catedral, un impresionante ejemplo del arte barroco, se levanta sobre los cimientos de un antiguo monasterio de la época carolingia. La biblioteca del convento, situada al lado, contiene toda una serie de valiosos documentos de la Edad Media, escritos a mano.

ST. GALLUS
A.D. 612

Im hügeligen **Appenzellerland,** südlich von St. Gallen, leben die schönen, alten Volksbräuche heute noch fort. Hier kann man die Talbewohner in ihren typischen, farbenprächtigen Trachten, folkloristische Alpaufzüge und riesige Kuhglocken bewundern, die für diese Gegend charakteristisch sind.

En **Appenzell,** pays de collines situé au sud de St-Gall, les belles coutumes populaires subsistent encore aujourd'hui. On peut y admirer le costume haut en couleurs de ses habitants, la montée à l'alpage folklorique et les gigantesques cloches de vaches, typiques de la région.

In hilly **Appenzell** country to the south of St. Gallen, the people have managed to keep their picturesque old folklore alive to this day. Here, you can still admire the valley-dwellers in their typical, colourful costumes, with their mountain attire and huge cow-bells which are so characteristic of this region.

La montuosa campagna dell'**Appenzello,** a sud di S. Gallo, è una regione dove vengono tuttora praticate le antiche e pittoresche tradizioni. Nei tipici e sgargianti costumi, gagliardi valligiani si esibiscono con gli enormi campanacci caratteristici di questa zona.

En la región de **Appenzell,** llena de colinas, situada al sur de San Gall, sobreviven las bellas y antiguas tradiciones populares. Aqui es posible admirar los habitantes del valle en sus trajes tipicos multicolor, los desplazamientos folkloristicos a los Alpes y enormes campanas de vacas que tan caracteristicas son de esta región.

An der berühmten Appenzeller Landsgemeinde kann der Bürger unmittelbar Einfluss auf die
Regierung seines Heimatkantons nehmen.

*Le célèbre Landsgemeinde d'Appenzel, où le cito-
yen participe directement à la direction de la
chose publique.*

*Each (male) citizen can directly influence the
government of his home canton by voting at
the famous Appenzell Landesgemeinde or Regional Community Meeting.*

*Il famoso Landsgemeinde di Appenzello, dove
il cittadino partecipa direttamente al governo
della cosa pubblica.*

*El ciudadano puede influenciar directamente
las decisiones del Gobierno de su cantón en
las famosas «Landsgemeinde».*

Typische Appenzeller Häuser mit ihren fröhlichen buntbemalten Fassaden.

Maisons appenzelloises typiques, aux façades agrémentées de peintures multicolores.

Typical Appenzell houses with their jolly, bright painted facades.

Le tipiche case di Appenzello, dalle facciate allegre e multicolori.

Tipicas casas de Appenzell, con sus fachadas pintadas en colores muy llamativos.

Eine Schwebebahn klettert von der **Schwägalp** auf den 2501 m hohen **Säntisgipfel,** auf dem man eine moderne, mit allem Komfort ausgestattete Unterkunft findet.

Un téléphérique monte de la **Schwägalp** au sommet du **Säntis,** à 2501 m d'altitude, où se trouve un établissement hôtelier moderne et confortable.

A cable-car climbs from the **Schwägalp** to the **Säntis Peak** at 8128 feet where the visitor is received in a modern hotel offering every form of comfort.

La vetta del Säntis, m. 25(raggiungibile con la funiv **Schwägalp.** Vi si trova un derno rifugio con ogni con

Un teleférico permite llega **Schwägalp** a la cumbre **Säntis,** situada a 2501 n altitud, donde se encuentr refugio moderno equipado el máximo confort.

Südlich vom Alpstein zeichnet sich das charakteristische Profil der **Churfirsten** ab.

Al sur de Alpstein se diseña el característico perfil de los **Churfirsten**.

The characteristic profile of the **Churfirsten** Range rises to the south of Alpstein.

A sud dell'Alpestein si erge il caratteristico profilo del **Churfirsten.**

Au sud de l'Alpstein se dessine la silhouette caractéristique des **Churfirsten.**

pperswil auch Rosenstadt genannt, liegt in einer herrlichen cht am Zürichsee. Von hier führt auch eine Dammstrasse er den See.

pperswil est située au bord du lac de Zurich, à l'endroit où e chaussée relie les deux berges du lac.

pperswil lies on the Lake of Zurich just where a long ncrete dyke joins the opposite shores.

pperswil è situata sul lago di Zurigo nel punto dove un go ponte-diga unisce le due sponde.

pperswil se encuentra a orillas del lago de Zurich, en el gar donde una carretera construida sobre terraplén une bas orillas.

Die tausendjährige Benediktiner-Abtei **Einsiedeln** ist das eindrücklichste Zeugnis barocker Baukunst in der Schweiz und einer der grossen Wallfahrtsorte Europas.

Einsiedeln, l'abbaye de bénédictins millénaire, est le témoignage le plus important de l'art baroque en Suisse et un des hauts lieux de pèlerinage du continent.

The thousand-year-old Benedictine Abbey at **Einsiedeln** is the most impressive example of baroque architecture in Switzerland and one of the main places of pilgrimage in Europe.

La millenaria abbazia benedettina di **Einsiedeln**, l'edificio barocco più significativo della Svizzera, meta di pellegrinaggio e devozione per la Madonna Nera.

La abadía de los benedictinos de **Einsiedeln**, construida hace unos mil años, es el más impresionante testimonio del estilo barroco en Suiza y uno de los lugares de peregrinación más concurridos de Europa.

Zug und Schwyz sind die Hauptstädte der beiden gleichnamigen Kantone. Zug ist der kleinste der Kantone, Schwyz derjenige, von dem die Schweiz ihren Namen ableitete.

Zoug et Schwyz sont les chefs-lieux des cantons de même nom. Zoug est le plus petit canton, Schwyz celui dont la Suisse a dérivé son nom.

Zug and Schwyz are each the capital of a canton of the same name. Zug is the smallest canton in Switzerland and Schwyz is that which gave the country its name.

Zug e Schwyz sono i capoluoghi dei rispettivi cantoni. Zug è il più piccolo dei cantoni, Schwyz è quello dal quale deriva il nome della Svizzera. Entrambe le città sono importanti centri industriali e turistici.

Zug y Schwyz son las capitales de ambos cantones del mismo nombre. Zug es el cantón más pequeño, y de Schwyz procede el nombre de Suiza.

Brunnen ist ein bekannter Kur- und Badeort am Ufer des Urnersees. Auf der gegenüberliegenden Seite liegt die **Rütliwiese,** auf welcher der erste Bund der Eidgenossenschaft geschlossen wurde.

Brunnen est une station thermale et balnéaire connue, située au bord du lac d'Uri. Sur le côté opposé se trouve la **prairie du Grütli,** où fut conclue la première alliance des Confédérés.

Brunnen is a famous spa on the banks of the Lake of Uri. Across the Lake is the Meadow of **Rütli** where the first Confederates took their oath of allegiance.

Brunnen, sulla riva dell'Urnersee, è un rinomato luogo di cura e bagni termali. Sull'altra sponda del lago si affaccia la **Ruetliwiese,** luogo di drammatici eventi storici.

Brunnen es un conocido centro de vacaciones y balnearios situado a orillas del Urnersee. En el lado opuesto se encuentra la «**Rütliwiese**» (Prado de Rütli), en el que se decidió la primera unión de la Confederación.

An der **Axenstrasse,** von der man eine wunderschöne Aussicht auf den Vierwaldstättersee geniesst, liegt die **Tellskapelle.**

La **route de l'Axen** offre un magnifique coup d'œil sur le lac des Quatre-Cantons. Sur son parcours se trouve la **chapelle de Tell.**

The **Tell Chapel** is located on the **Axenstrasse** from where you can enjoy a beautiful view of the Lake of Lucerne.

La Tellskapelle si trova lungo la **Axenstrasse,** una delle strade panoramiche più suggestive sul Lago dei Quattro Cantoni.

En la **Axenstrasse,** que tiene maravillosas vistas sobre el Lago de los Cuatro Cantones, se encuentra la **Capilla de Guillermo Tell.**

Altdorf, der Hauptort des Kantons Uri; hier soll Wilhelm Tell seinen berühmten Apfelschuss getan haben.

Altdorf, chef-lieu du canton d'Uri; c'est en ce lieu que Tell aurait transpercé la fameuse pomme.

Altdorf the capital of the Canton of Uri is the place where William Tell is purported to have fired his famous shot at the apple.

Altdorf, il capoluogo del Cantone di Uri, patria dell'eroe nazionale Guglielmo Tell, è la culla della storia e della civiltà svizzera.

Altdorf, la capital del cantón Uri; según la leyenda, fue aquí donde Guillermo Tell realizó su famoso disparo con flecha a la manzana colocada sobre la cabeza de su hijo.

Luzern ist die Hauptstadt des gleichnamigen Kantons. Das Wahrzeichen der Stadt ist die um 1300 erbaute Kapellbrücke über die Reuss, die älteste gedeckte Holzbrücke Europas. Ebenso grosser Bekanntheit erfreut sich der achteckige Wasserturm.

Lucerne est le chef-lieu du canton de meme nom. La caractéristique de la ville est la Kapellbrücke, qui fut construite vers 1300 sur la Reuss; c'est le plus ancien pont couvert d'Europe. Le Wasserturm octogonal est également familier.

Lucerne is the capital of the Canton of the same name. The landmark of the town is the Chapel Bridge built over the River Reuss around 1300. This is the oldest covered wooden bridge in Europe. The octagonal water tower is equally famous.

Lucerna è il capoluogo dell'omonimo Cantone. Il suo caratteristico distintivo è il «Kapellbrücke», il ponte di legno costruito nel 1333 che attraversa il fiume «Reuss». Altrettanto nota è la ottagonale Torre dell'Acqua.

Lucerna es la capital del cantón del mismo nombre. El símbolo de la ciudad es el «Kapellbrücke» (Puente de la Capilla), construido en 1300 sobre el rio Reuss. Se trata del puente de madera cubierto más antiguo de Europa. También ha adquirido gran fama la Torre de agua octogonal.

Majestätisch thront über der Stadt Luzern der **Pilatus**, ein beliebtes Ausflugsziel. Auf der gegenüberliegenden Seeseite erhebt sich das **Rigimassiv**.

Le **Pilate**; but d'excursion apprécié, domine fièrement la ville de Lucerne. Sur la rive opposée du lac s'élève le massif du **Righi**.

Mount **Pilatus** rises majestically over Lucerne and offers a favourite outing spot. Across the Lake may be seen the **Rigi** Mountain.

La città è dominata dalla imponente massa del monte **Pilatus,** una delle mete preferite dal visitatore. Dal lato opposto, il gruppo del **Rigi**.

El monte **Pilato**, meta muy apreciada de excursiones, se alza majestuoso sobre la ciudad de Lucerna. En el lado opuesto del lago se encuentra el macizo **Rigi**.

Der **Bürgenstock** ist eine heitere Hochebene üb[er] dem Vierwaldstättersee.

Le **Bürgenstock** est un haut plateau dégagé, sit[ué] au-dessus du lac des Quatre-Cantons, à 874 m d'a[lti]tude.

The **Bürgstock** is a bright plateau hanging 2840 fe[et] above the Lake of Lucerne.

Il **Bürgenstock** è un ridente pianoro che si affaccia s[ul] lago a m. 874 d'altezza.

El **Bürgenstock** es una encantadora altiplanicie situa[da] a 874 m de altura sobre el Lago de los Cuat[ro] Cantones.

Luzern hat ein reiches künstlerisches und kulturelles Leben. Jahr für Jahr ziehen die internationalen Musikfestwochen eine grosse Zahl von Besuchern an. Eine Schiffahrt auf dem See ist ein unvergessliches Erlebnis.

Lucerne connaît une riche vie artistique et culturelle. Chaque année, les Semaines internationales de musique attirent un grand nombre de mélomanes. Une croisière sur le lac reste un évènement inoubliable.

Lucerne enjoys a rich artistic and cultural life. Year after year, the International Music Festival draws large numbers of visitors. A boat trip on the lake is an unforgettable experience.

Lucerna ha una ricca vita artistica e culturale, molti visitatori accorrono ogni anno ai suoi Festival Musicali Internazionali. Una gita sul lago è un'esperienza affascinante ed indimenticabile.

Lucerna cuenta con una rica vida artística y cultural. Las Semanas Musicales Internacionales atraen cado año gran número de visitantes. Un viaje en barco sobre el lago constituye un acontecimiento inolvidable.

s Hotel Kulm auf dem 2132 m hohen **Pila-**
s. Von diesem Aussichtsberg geniesst man
en herrlichen Ueberblick auf Luzern und
n unteren Teil des Vierwaldstättersees. Er
 mit einer kühnen Schwebebahn oder der
nnradbahn bequem zu erreichen.

Hotel Kulm on Mount **Pilatus** which rises to
10,200 feet. A fantastic view of Lucerne and
the lower end of its Lake is visible from the
slopes of this mountain. The peak is easily
reached by a breathtaking suspended cable-
car or a more sedate rack-railway.

El hotel Kulm en el **Monte Pilato**, a 2132 m de
altitud. Desde este monte panorámico se tie-
nen unas vistas maravillosas de Lucerna y de
la parte inferior del Lago de los Cuatro
Cantones. El acceso al mismo se encuentra
asegurado mediante un teleférico de atrevida
construcción o bien por un ferrocarril de cremallera.

ôtel Kulm, sur le **Pilate**, altitude 2132 m. Ce
mmet offre une vue splendide sur Lucerne
la partie inférieure du lac des Quatre-Can-
s. Il est facilement accessible par un télé-
érique audacieusement implanté ou par le
emin de fer à crémaillère.

L'Hotel Kulm sul **Monte Pilatus** (m. 2132), dal
quale si può ammirare il panorama di Lucerna
e della parte inferiore del Lago dei Quattro
Cantoni. È collegato a Lucerna da un'ardita
funivia ed una ferrovia a cremagliera.

Brienz ist das Tor zum Berner Oberland. Von hier fährt man mit der Zahnradbahn auf das Brienzer Rothorn.

Brienz est la porte de l'Oberland bernois. De ce lieu, un chemin de fer à crémaillère monte au Rothorn de Brienz.

Brienz is the gate to the Bernese Highlands. From here, the rack railway will take you up the Brienzer Rothorn.

Brienz è la prima tappa dell'Oberland Bernese. Da qui si sale al Rothorn con una ferrovia a cremagliera.

Brienz es la puerta de entrada al Oberland Bernés. Desde aquí, se puede acceder al Brienzer Rothorn mediante el ferrocarril de cremallera.

Das imposante **Jungfraumassiv** ist das Wahrzeichen der Region. Der von ewigem Schnee bedeckte Gipfel erreicht eine Höhe von 4166 m.

L'imposant massif de la **Jungfrau** caractérise la région. Le sommet aux neiges éternelles s'élève à 4166 m d'altitude.

The impressive **Jungfrau** Mountain is the local landmark. The peak, constantly swathed in snow, rises to 13,540 feet.

L'imponente massiccio della **Jungfrau** è la montagna più rappresentativa della regione. La sua vetta, coperta da nevi esterne, raggiunge i m. 4166.

El imponente macizo **Jungfrau** constituye el simbolo de la región. La cumbre, cubierta con nieve perpetua, llega a una altitud de 4166 m.

Grindelwald

Interlaken ist der Ausgangspunkt für unvergessliche Wanderungen in die umliegende Bergwelt. Zu den schönsten Ausflugszielen gehören die **Kleine Scheidegg**, das **Jungfraujoch**, das **Schilthorn** und die **Schynige Platte**.

Interlaken est le point de départ de randonnées inoubliables dans les montagnes environnantes. Parmi les plus beaux buts d'excursion, il faut mentionner la **Petite Scheidegg**, le **Jungfraujoch**, le **Schilthorn** et la **Schynige Platte**.

Interlaken is the starting point for many an unforgettable hike into the surrounding mountainside. Among the most beautiful places to visit are the **Kleine Scheidegg**, the **Jungfraujoch**, the **Schilthorn** and the **Schynige Platte**.

Interlaken è la base di partenza per meravigliose escursioni nella regione. Tra le cime più belle sono la **Kleine Scheidegg** ed il **Wetterhorn** a **Grindelwald**.

Interlaken es el punto de partida de inolvidables excursiones en el mundo montañoso de los alrededores. Entre los más bellos destinos de excursiones se encuentran el **Kleine Scheidegg**, **Jungfraujoch**, **Schilthorn** y **Schynige Platte**.

Im ewigen Schnee des **Jungfraujochs** kann man sich von den berühmten «Husky»- Schlittenhunden durch den Schnee ziehen lassen. 3573 m ü. M. steht die «Sphinx» genannte Wetterwarte.

Au **Jungfraujoch**, des ballades en traîneau dans les neiges éternelles, avec les fameux chiens polaires husky, attendent le visiteur. A 3573 m d'altitude se trouve la station météorologique nommée «Sphinx».

The famous husky sledge dogs will take you skimming through the eternal snow on the **Jungfraujoch**. At an altitude of 11,612 feet is the meteorological station known as the «Sphinx».

Sulle nevi della **Jungfrau** è possibile compiere escursioni su slitte trainate dai famosi cani polari «Husky». A quota m. 3573 si trova l'Osservatorio meteorologico denominato «Sfinge».

En la nieve eterna del **Jungfraujoch** se pueden ver los famosos perros «Husky» que tiran de los trineos. El observatorio meteorológico, conocido con el nombre de «Esfinge», se encuentra a 3573 m de altitud sobre el nivel del mar.

Die Jungfraubahn ist eine grosse Attraktion. Sie führt den Besucher bis unter den Gipfel, auf eine Höhe von 3454 m. Der Bahnhof ist stollenartig in den Fels gehauen und gewährt direkten Zugang zu einem Hotel-Restaurant.

Le chemin de fer de la Jungfrau est particulièrement attractif. Il conduit jusque sous le sommet, à une altitude de 3454 m. La gare est creusée en galerie dans le rocher et donne directement accès à un hôtel-restaurant.

The Jungfrau Railway is a great attraction. It carries visitors up to 11,226 feet, just below the peak. The station has been hewed out of the rock and provides direct access to a hotel/restaurant.

La ferrovia della Jungfrau è una grande attrazione. Essa porta i visitatori sotto la vetta del monte a quota m. 3454. La stazione è scavata in una galleria da dove si accede direttamente ad un albergo ristorante.

El ferrocarril de la Jungfrau es una gran atracción. Lleva al visitante a una altitud de 3454 m, a poca distancia de la cumbre de la Jungfrau. La estación ha sido construida en forma de galería en la roca, y permite el acceso directo a un hotel-restaurante.

Ein stimmungsvoller Sonnenuntergang.

Féerie d'un coucher de soleil.

The setting sun also sets the mood.

Nella suggestiva luce del tramonto...

Una puesta de sol impresionante.

Im **Lauterbrunnental** offenbart sich die Alpenwelt mit ihren hohen Wasserfällen und senkrechten Felswänden über den Dörfern in ihrer ganzen Schönheit.

Dans la **vallée de Lauterbrunnen**, l'univers alpestre se manifeste dans toute sa splendeur, avec ses chutes d'eau et ses parois verticales dominant les villages.

In the **Lauterbrunnental** the Alps come into their full glory with their towering waterfalls and vertical cliffs dropping down to the villages below.

La **Lauterbrunnental** offre uno splendido paesaggio alpino, con alte cascate d'acqua e pareti a picco sui villaggi.

El mundo de los Alpes, con sus altas cascadas y verticales paredes rocosas sobre los pueblos, se ofrece en toda su belleza en el **Lauterbrunnental**.

Von **Mürren** aus ste Schwebebahn auf 2971 m hohe Sch das auch unter de men Piz Gloria beka

De **Mürren**, le téléph monte au Schilthorn mé également Piz G 2971 m d'altitude.

The cable car sets ou **Mürren** and climbs 9656-foot-high Sch which is also known Piz Gloria.

A **Mürren** la funivia Schilthorn sale fino 2971 sul Piz Gloria

Desde **Mürren**, el te co sube al Schilkth tuado a 2971 m de conocido con el nom Piz Gloria.

Schilthorn

Thun mit seinem charakteristischen mittelalterlichen Schloss blickt auf den Thunersee.

Thoune, avec son château moyenâgeux caractéristique, se mire dans le lac de Thoune.

Thun with its characteristic castle from the
Middle Ages overlooking the Lake of Thun.

Thun, con il caratteristico castello medievale,
si affaccia sul lago omonimo.

Thun, con su caracteristico castillo de la Edad
Media, tiende su vista sobre el lago de Thun.

Schönried mit dem Rü-
blihorn im Hintergrund.

Schönried avec le Rü-
blihorn à l'arrière-plan.

Schönried with the
Rüblihorn in the
background.

Schönried a m. 12
con il Rublihorn s
sfondo.

Schönried, con el
blihorn al fondo.

Das Palace Hotel in **Gstaad,** einem exklusiven und mondänen Ferienort im Saanenland.

Le Palace Hôtel de **Gstaad**, lieu privilégié des vacances mondaines, dans la contrée de Saanen.

The Palace Hotel in **Gstaad**, an exclusive and fashionable holiday resort in the Saanen region.

Il Palace Hotel a **Gstaad,** esclusivo e mondano luogo di villeggiatura dello Saanenland.

El Hotel Palace en **Gstaad**, un centro exclusivo y mundano de vacaciones en Saanenland.

Zweisimmen

Das Gifferhorn und der Wasserngrat über **Saanen.**

Le Gifferhorn et le Wasserngrat, au-dessus de **Saanen.**

The Gifferhorn and the Wasserngrat above **Saanen.**

Il Gifferhorn ed il Wasserngrat a **Saanen.**

El Gifferhorn y el Wasserngrat sobre **Saanen.**

Hoch ragt der Turm des gotischen Münsters über die Dächer **Berns**. In der Hauptstadt der Schweiz befinden sich das Bundeshaus, Sitz der Landesregierung, das Parlament und verschiedene nationale Verwaltungsstellen.

La tour du Münster gothique s'élance au-dessus des toits de **Berne**. La capitale de la Suisse a été fondée en 1191, et on y trouve le Palais fédéral, siège du gouvernement national, le Parlement et diverses administrations fédérales.

The tower of the Gothic Minster rises high above the rooftops of **Bern**. Here, in the capital of Switzerland, founded in 1191, is the Federal Palace, the seat of the National Government, the Parliament and various administrative offices.

Sovrastata dall'alto campanile gotico della cattedrale, **Berna**, fondata nel 1191, è la capitale della Svizzera. Qui si trovano il Palazzo federale, sede del governo centrale, il Parlamento ed altri uffici amministrativi nazionali.

La torre de la catedral gótica sobresale a gran altura sobre los tejados de **Berna**. En la capital de Suiza, fundada en 1191, se encuentran el «Bundeshaus» – sede del Gobierno de los Estados –, el Parlamento y diferentes oficinas de administración nacionales.

Kunstvolle Brunnen mit farbenprächtigen Standbildern und die Arkaden, Lauben genannt, prägen das Bild der Altstadt. Der Bärengraben und der Zeitglockenturm zählen zu den Wahrzeichen von Bern.

La vieille ville se caractérise par ses fontaines artistement construites, surmontées de statues colorées, et ses arcades, ou galeries. La fosse aux ours et la tour de l'Horloge sont des images bien connues de Berne.

The Old Town derives its character from the many delightful fountains adorned by colourful statues and from the arcades-known as Lauben. The Bear Pit and the Clock Tower – the Zytglokke – are just two of the landmarks of Bern.

Artistiche e colorate fontane, torri imponenti, i "Portici", caratterizzano la città vecchia e le conferiscono un'atmosfera cordiale ed intima.

Unas fuentes artisticas con estatuas llenas de colorido, así como las Arcadas, conocidas con el nombre de «Lauben», caracterizan la imagen de la parte antigua de la ciudad. El Foso de los Osos y la «Zeitglockenturm» (Torre con Campanas y Reloj) son algunos de los simbolos caracteristicos de Berna.

Schloss Erlach am Ende des Bielersees ist umgeben von gepflegten Weinbergen.

Le **château de Cerlier**, à l'extrémité du lac de Bienne, est environné de vignobles soignés.

Erlach Castle at the end of the Lake of Biel is surrounded by carefully tended vineyards.

Il **Castello di Erlach** è situato nella parte terminale del lago di Biel, contornato da vigneti di qualità.

El **castillo Erlach** en el extremo del lago de Biel, está rodeado de viñedos muy bien cuidados.

Solothurn ist die Hauptstad gleichnamigen Kantons. Die deren Gründung auf römische zurückgeht, liegt am Ufer der A der Altstadt sind zahlreiche S würdigkeiten zu bewundern.

Soleure est le chef-lieu du can même nom. La ville, dont la for remonte au temps des Romain située sur les rives de l'Aar. La ville contient de nombreuses sités remarquables.

Solothurn is the capital of the of the same name. The town, was founded back in Roman time on the banks of the Aare. Th Town has much worth seeing.

Soletta è la capitale dell'om Cantone. Situata sul fiume Aare origine romana. La città vecchia di monumenti.

Solothurn es la capital del cant mismo nombre. La ciudad, cuya ción se remonta a la época romanos, está situada a orillas Aar. En la parte antigua de la pueden admirarse numerosas c dades dignas de ver.

Die am Fusse des Juras gelegene Stadt **Biel** besitzt eine traditionelle Uhrenindustrie.

La ville de **Bienne**, *située au pied du Jura, possède une industrie horlogère traditionnelle.*

Biel/Bienne is a small town at the foot of the Jura Mountains, known for its traditional watch and clock-making industry.

Bienne *è città di origine celtica, situata ai piedi del Giura. Vi fiorisce l'industria dell'orologio.*

La ciudad **Biel**, situada a los pies de la cadena montañosa del Jura, cuenta con una industria relojera tradicional.

Schloss Burgdorf

Neuenburg ist die Hauptstad[t] des gleichnamigen Kantons. Die Stadt erstreckt sich a[m] Fusse des Juras, in bevorzug[ter] Lage am See und ist reic[h] an Baudenkmälern aus der Re[n]aissance und dem Barock.

Neuchâtel est le chef-lieu d[u] canton de même nom. La vill[e] occupe une situation privilé[giée] en bordure du lac, au pie[d] du Jura, et possède un riche patrimoine architectural de l[a] Renaissance et du baroque.

Neuchatel is the capital of the canton of the same name. The town lies at the foot of the Jur[a] Mountains in a splendid lake

de location and is rich in
Renaissance and Baroque mo-
uments.

Neuchâtel è la capitale del-
omonimo cantone. Situata ai
edi del Giura, in bellissima
osizione sul lago, essa è ric-
a di edifici rinascimentali e
arocchi.

Neuenburg es la capital del
cantón del mismo nombre. La
iudad se extiende a los pies
el Jura, está situada en un
gar privilegiado del lago y es
ca en edificios del
enacimiento y del barroco.

Murten ist ein von Mauern
umschlossenes mittelalterli-
ches Städtchen. Gut erhalten
sind das Schloss aus dem 13.
bis 16. Jh. und die Wehranla-
gen.

Morat est une petite ville
moyenâgeuse, entourée de
murailles. Le château construit
du XIIIe au XVIe siècle et les
fortifications sont bien conser-
vés.

Murten/Morat is a small, wal-
led city of the Middle Ages.
The Castle (13th to 16th centuries) and battlements have
been well preserved.

Murten è un'antica città medievale fortificata. Ancora bene
conservati sono il castello del
XIII secolo ed i bastioni.

Morat es una pequeña ciudad
de la Edad Media, rodeada de
murallas. Se encuentran en
perfecto estado el castillo
construido del siglo XIII al XVI,
y también las instalaciones
defensivas.

▼

Freiburg ist die Hauptstadt des gleichnamigen Kantons. Der malerische alte Stadtkern, der noch immer von Mauern umschlossen ist, drängt sich um die Kathedrale St-Nicolas.

Fribourg est le chef-lieu du canton de même nom. Le centre ancien, pittoresque, a conservé ses murailles et se serre autour de la cathédrale St-Nicolas.

Freiburg is the capital of the canton of the same name. The picturesque heart of the Old Town, clustered around the foot of St. Nicholas' Cathedral, is still encompassed by its city walls.

Friburgo è il capoluogo del cantone omonimo. Il nucleo più antico e pittoresco ancora cinto di mura, si stringe intorno alla cattedrale di S. Nicola.

Friburgo es la capital del cantón del mismo nombre. El pintoresco núcleo de la parte antigua de la ciudad, rodeado todavia de murallas, se extiende alrededor de la catedral San Nicolás.

Die Gegend um **Gruyères,** einem idyllischen Städtchen, ist die Heimat des bekannten Greyerzer Käses.

La région de **Gruyères,** une cité idyllique, est la patrie du fameux fromage.

The area around **Gruyère,** a little dream of a town, is the home of the well-known Gruyère cheese.

Gruyère, nella bassa valle della Sarine, è la patria del famoso formaggio.

La región alrededor de **Gruyères,** perqueña ciudad idílica, es el lugar de donde procede el conocido queso de Gruyère.

Lausanne, die Hauptstadt des Kantons Waadt, ist die zweitgrösste Stadt der Westschweiz. Die am Lac Léman gelegene Metropole mit ihrem reichen künstlerischen und kulturellen Leben ist zugleich ein blühendes Zentrum des Handels und der Industrie.

Lausanne, chef-lieu du canton de Vaud, est la seconde ville de Suisse romande. Cette métropole des rives du Léman, qui connaît une riche animation artistique et culturelle, est également un centre de commerce et d'industrie florissant.

Lausanne is the capital of the canton of Vaud and is the second largest town in French-speaking Switzerland. This city on Lake Leman enjoys a rich artistic and cultural life and, at the same time, is a thriving centre of trade and industry.

Losanna, capoluogo del Cantone di Vaud, è una delle due metropoli romande. Città ricca di fascino con una grande vita artistica e culturale; vi fioriscono anche il commercio e l'industria.

Lausana, capital del cantón de Vaud, es la segunda ciudad en importancia de la Suiza occidental. Esta metrópoli, situada a orillas del lago de Ginebra, con su rica vida artística y cultural, es un próspero centro del comercio y de la industria.

Die Kathedrale aus dem 12. und 13.
Jh. ist das bedeutendste Bauwerk der
Frühgotik in der Schweiz. Das Schloss
St-Maire aus dem 15. Jh. ist heute Sitz
der Kantonsregierung.

La cathédrale des XIIe et XIIIe siècles
est le principal édifice du gothique pri-
mitif en Suisse. Le château St-Maire,
du XVe siècle, abrite actuellement le
gouvernement cantonal.

The Cathedral, from the 12th and 13th
centuries, is one of the main early Gothic buildings in Switzerland. St. Mary's
castle, a 15th century structure, today
houses the Cantonal Government.

La cattedrale del XII secolo è uno dei
più significativi edifici gotici della Svizzera. Il castello del XIV-XV secolo è
sede del governo cantonale.

La catedral, construida en los siglos
XII y XIII, es la obra más importante del
arte gótico primario en Suiza. El castillo St-Maire, del siglo XV, es actualmente la sede del Gobierno cantonal.

Der Springbrunnen mit seinem
130 m hohen Wasserstrahl ist
weltberühmt. Zahlreiche Gär-
ten und Parkanlagen mit einer
Vielfalt von Blumen und Pflan-
zen säumen die Bucht, und
majestätisch erheben sich im
Hintergrund die Alpen.

Le jet d'eau de 130 m est connu dans le monde entier. D'in-
nombrables parcs et jardins
d'une grande richesse bordent
la rade, et les Alpes s'élèvent
majestueusement à l'arrière-
plan.

The fountain with its column of
water rising to over 423 feet is
world-famous. Many gardens
and parks, alive with all manner
of flowers and plants, dot the
bay and stand out against the
majestic background of the
Alps.

La fontana nell'acqua con il
suo getto di m. 130, è nota in
tutto il mondo. Lungo la baia si
affacciano numerosi giardini e
parchi ricchi di fiori e piante, e
sullo sfondo dominano imponenti le Alpi.

El surtidor de agua, con su
chorro de agua de 130 m de
altura, ha adquirido fama mun-
dial. Numerosos jardines y par-
ques con innumerables flores
y plantas embellecen la bahia;
al fondo se elevan majestuosos los Alpes.

A l'extrémité ouest du lac Léman se trouve **Genève**, deuxiè-
me ville de Suisse et chef-lieu
du canton de même nom. Habi-
tée depuis le néolithique, elle
devint, grâce à sa situation
géographique propice, oppidum celte puis capitale bur-
gonde. Centre de la Réforme
calviniste depuis le XVIe siècle, Genève entra dans la Con-
fédération helvétique en 1815
et, de par sa vocation interna-
tionale, elle acquit bientôt un
rôle d'envergure.

At the western end of the Lake
of Geneva, lies the second
biggest city in Switzerland –
Geneva – which is the capital
of the canton of the same
name. A settlement has existed
on this site since the early
Stone Age and, because of its
favorable geographical location it became the site of a
Celtic township and later the
capital of the Burgundian
Kingdom. It has been the centre of Calvanist reform since
the 16th century and, in 1815,
it joined the Swiss Confedera-
tion and soon started to play an
important role through its international vocation.

Sulle rive del capo occidentale
del lago Lemano sorge la se-
conda maggiore città della
Svizzera, **Ginevra**, capitale del-
l'omonimo cantone. Abitata già
in età antica grazie alla sua
favorevole posizione geografi-
ca, fu poi città romana ed im-
periale. Ginevra entra nella
confederazione elvetica del
1815 e subito, per la sua voca-
zione internazionale, vi svolge
un ruolo determinante.

En el extremo occidental del
lago de Ginebra se encuentra
la segunda ciudad en importancia de Suiza, **Ginebra**, capital del cantón del mismo nombre. Poblada desde el Neolíti-
co, y debido a su favorable si-
tuación geográfica, fue el lugar
de un «Oppidum» celta, y más
tarde capital del reino de Bor-
goña. Centro de la Reforma
calvinista desde el siglo XVI,
Ginebra ingresó en la Confederación suiza en 1815 y, a
través de su visión internacional, adquirió muy pronto un papel líder.

Genf, die Heimatstadt Calvins, hat in der Religionsgeschichte Westeuropas eine führende Rolle gespielt. Der Einfluss des nahen Frankreichs ist deutlich zu spüren, und seit jeher kennzeichnen Weltoffenheit und Menschlichkeit den Geist dieser Stadt.

Genève, ville d'adoption de Calvin, a joué un rôle important dans l'histoire des religions de l'Europe occidentale. L'influence de la France voisine se ressent nettement et, depuis toujours, la ville est connue pour son ouverture au monde et son esprit humanitaire.

Geneva, the home-town of Calvin, played a leading role in the religious history of Europe. This town has, since its earliest days, been outward-looking and humanitarian in spirit and the influence of neighbouring France is here all too apparent.

Patria di Calvino, Ginevra, è uno dei centri protagonisti dei destini religiosi dell'Europa occidentale. Sotto l'influenza della vicina Francia, essa è da sempre animata da un grande spirito aperto ed umanitario.

Ginebra, ciudad natal de Calvino, ha jugado un papel muy importante en la historia religiosa de la Europa Occidental. Se percibe claramente la influencia de la cercana Francia, y esta ciudad se caracteriza, desde los primeros tiempos, por su cosmopolitismo y carácter humanitario.

CALVIN

FAREL

1559

itten im Bourg de Four steht
e im 12. Jh. erbaute Kathe-
ale St-Pierre, das Wahrzei-
en der Altstadt.

a cathédrale St-Pierre, édi-
ée au XIIe siècle à proximité
u Bourg-de-Four, caractérise
 vieille ville.

 the centre of the Bourg du
our stands the landmark of
e Old Town, St. Peter's
athedral, built in the 12th
entury.

La cattedrale di S. Pietro, co-
struita nel dodicesimo secolo,
si erge nel bel mezzo del
Bourg de Four e costituisce
l'emblema della città vecchia.

En el centro del «Bourg de
Four» se encuentra la catedral
St-Pierre, construida en el siglo XII y que es actualmente
un símbolo de la parte antigua
de la ciudad.

Seine lange Tradition als Hort der Freiheit und Menschlichkeit machen Genf zu einem idealen Verhandlungsort. Hier, auf neutralem Boden, treffen sich die Völker der ganzen Welt, hier steht der **Völkerbundspalast,** in dem Entscheide von internationaler Bedeutung gefällt werden – worauf auch die «Manship-Kugel» hinzuweisen scheint.

La longue tradition de Genève comme cité de liberté et d'humanisme en fait le lieu de négociations idéal. Les peuples du monde entier s'y rencontrent sur territoire neutre; on y trouve le **palais des Nations**, où sont prises d'importantes décisions sur le plan international, symbolisées, semble-t-il, par la sphère Manship du palais.

Its long tradition as a stronghold of freedom and humanity has made Geneva an ideal place for meeting and negotiating. Here, on neutral ground, the people from the four corners of the world meet and discuss, here is located the **Palais des Nations** where decisions of international importance are taken – as the «Armilliary sphere» would seem to indicate.

Per le sue grandi tradizioni di libertà ed umanità, Ginevra è per natura la sede dove i vari popoli del mondo, in terra neutrale, si costituiscono in comunità. Qui sorge infatti il **Palazzo delle Nazioni,** dove prendono corpo i destini del mondo, come quasi è dato d'intuire nella «Sfera di Manship».

Su larga tradición como cuna de la libertad y carácter humanitario hacen de Ginebra un lugar ideal de negociaciones. Aquí, en un terreno neutral, se reúnen los representantes de todo el mundo, y es también aquí donde se encuentra el **Palacio de las Naciones Unidas,** en el que se toman decisiones de transcendencia internacional.

Die **Waadtländer Riviera** am Genfersee ist gesäumt von malerischen Winzerdörfern mit gepflegten Weinbergen, kleinen Städtchen und reizenden Vergnügungshäfen. Dank dem günstigen Klima gedeihen hier die vorzüglichen Lavaux-Reben, aus denen man einen ausgezeichneten Weisswein gewinnt.

La **Riviera vaudoise** sur le lac Léman, est bordée de villages viticoles pittoresques aux vignobles soignés, de petites cités et de ports de plaisance charmants. Le climat favorise la croissance des cépages du Lavaux, qui produisent un vin blanc apprécié.

The **Vaud Riviera** on the Lake of Geneva is dotted with tiny, picturesque villages with their well-tended vineyards, little towns and delighful pleasure ports. The climate here is ideal for the excellent Lavaux vine from which a first rate white wine is produced.

La **Riviera Romana**, sul Lago Lemano, è punteggiata di pittoreschi villaggi ove si coltiva la vite, di piccole cittadine con incantevoli porti turistici. Grazie al clima della zona, le meravigliose vigne del Lavaux producono un ottimo vino bianco.

La **Riviera del país de Vaud** en el lago de Ginebra está bordada de pintorescos pueblos de cosecheros de uva que cultivan cuidadosamente los viñedos, de pequeñas ciudades y de encantadores puertos de recreo. El favorable clima de esta región permite que maduren bien las exquisitas vides de Lavaux, de las que se obtiene un excelente vino blanco.

Der Turm von **Marsens** das **Schloss Glérolles** in Waadtländer Weinbergen Genfersee.

La tour de **Marsens** et le teau de Glérolles, dans le gnobles vaudois, sur le Lé

Marsens Tower and **Glér Castle** among the Vaud yards on the shores of the of Geneva.

La torre di **Marsens e Cu** Castello di Glerolle.

La Torre de **Marsens** y el tillo Glèrolles en los viñ del pais de Vaud, a orilla lago de Ginebra.

Vevey, ein bezauberndes Städtchen mit Blick auf die majestätischen Savoyer Alpen.

Vevey, cité enchanteresse avec vue sur les imposantes Alpes de Savoie.

Vevey, a fascinating little town with a view of the majestic Savoy Alps.

Vevey, graziosa cittadina con a fronte le imponenti Alpi della Savoia francese.

Vevey, pequeña y encantadora ciudad con vistas a los majestuosos Alpes saboyanos.

Das **Schloss Blonay** oberhalb von Vevey. Die liebliche Bucht von **Montreux** wird von den hohen Wänden des Rochers-de-Naye beherrscht, der einen wunderbaren Rundblick über die ganze Waadtländerküste bietet. Im Hintergrund der Mont Pèlerin.

Le **château de Blonay** au-dessus de Vevey. La paisible baie de **Montreux** est dominée par les hautes parois des Rochers de Naye, sommets offrant une magnifique vue d'ensemble de la côte vaudoise. A l'arrière-plan, le Mont Pèlerin.

Blonay Castle overlooking Vevey. Charming **Montreux** bay at the foot of the towering Rochers-de-Naye the top of which offers a fantastic panorama of the entire Vaud coastal region. In the background, Mont Pèlerin.

Il **Castello di Blonay** - La bella baia di **Montreux** è sovrastata dalle alte pareti della montagna di Richer-de-Naye dalla quale si coglie un meraviglioso panorama su tutta la Riviera Romanda. Sullo sfondo il Mont Pelèrin.

El **castillo Blonay** encima de Vevey. La idílica bahía de **Montreux** está dominada por las altas paredes de Rocher-de-Naye, que ofrecen una maravillosa panorámica sobre toda la costa del país de Vaud. Al fondo puede verse el Mont Pèlerin.

Schloss Chillon steht auf einem Felsen am Ufer des Genfersees, in der Nähe von Montreux, und zählt zweifellos zu den berühmtesten Sehenswürdigkeiten der Schweiz. Zur Festung ausgebaut vom 11. bis ins 13. Jh., war es bis 1536 oft Wohnsitz der Grafen und Herzöge von Savoyen. In seinen Kerkern wurde Bonivard gefangen gehalten.

Le **château de Chillon** est construit sur un rocher des rives mêmes du Léman, près de Montreux, et compte assurément parmi les sites les plus célèbres de Suisse. Etabli comme forteresse du XIe au XIIIe siècle, les comtes et ducs de Savoie l'habitèrent souvent, et Bonivard fut tenu captif dans ses cachots.

Chillon Castle stands on a rocky outcrop overlooking the Lake of Geneva and not far from Montreux. It must be one of the most famous sites in Switzerland. It was developed from the 11th to the 13th century as a fortress and, until 1536, it often served as residence for the Counts and Dukes of Savoy. Bonivard was held prisoner in its dungeons.

Il **Castello di Chillon**, costruito su di una roccia in riva al lago nei pressi di Montreux, è forse il monumento più noto della Svizzera. Edificato da Pietro di Savoia nel XIII secolo, fu per secoli residenza favorita dei conti e dei duchi di questa Casa. Nelle sue celle fu tenuto prigioniero Bonivard.

El castillo de Chillon se encuentra sobre una roca situada a orillas del lago de Ginebra, a poca distancia de Montreux, y es indudablemente una de las curiosidades más dignas de ver de Suiza. Construido como fortaleza entre los siglos XI y XII, sirvió a menudo, hasta 1536, como residencia de los Condes y Duques de Saboya. Bonivard estuvo encerrado en sus calabozos.

Das aus dem 12. Jh. stammen-
de Schloss **Aigle** steht im Herzen eines blühenden Weinbau-
gebietes.

Le château d'**Aigle**, du XIIe siècle, est situé au cœur d'une
région viticole prospère.

Aigle Castle, a 12th century
construction, stands in the
heart of a thriving wine-growing
region.

Il **Castello di Aigle**, originario
del XII secolo, si trova al centro
di una zona di rigogliosi vigneti.

El castillo **Aigle**, construido en
el siglo XII, se encuentra en el
corazón de una floreciente región productora de vino.

Leysin

Verbier ist ein bekannter Ferienort auf einer Sonnenterrasse über dem Val de Bagnes.

Verbier, lieu de vacances connu, jouit d'une situation ensoleillée au-dessus du val de Bagnes.

Verbier is a well-known holiday resort in a sun-trap above the Val de Bagnes.

Verbier è un importante centro turistico della Val di Bagnes, a m. 1510 d'altezza.

Verbier es un conocido centro de vacaciones situado encima del Val de Bagnes sobre una terraza muy soleada.

Sitten ist die Hauptstadt des Kantons Wallis und Bischofssitz. Die Stadt wird von zwei Hügeln beherrscht, auf denen die befestigte Stiftskirche Notre-Dame-de-Valère und die Ueberreste der Bischofsburg Tourbillon aus dem 13. Jh. stehen.

Sion est le chef-lieu du canton du Valais et siège épiscopal. La ville est dominée par deux collines où se trouvent l'église fortifiée Notre-Dame-de-Valère et les ruines du château épiscopal de Tourbillon, du XIIIe siècle.

Sitten is the capital of the canton of Valais and a bishopric. The town is overshadowed by two hills crowned by the fortified monastery of Notre-Dame-de-Valère and the remains of the 13th century bishop's palace of Tourbillon.

Sion è la capitale del Vallese e sede vescovile. Essa è dominata da due colline sulle quali vi sono la chiesa fortificata di Notre Dame di Valère ed i resti di un castello episcopale originario del XIII secolo.

Sitten es la capital del cantòn del Valais y obispado. La ciudad està dominada por dos colinas en las que se encuentran los monasterios fortificados Notre-Dame-de-Valère y los restos de la fortaleza episcopal Tourbillon del siglo XIII.

Der Plaine-Morte Gletscher oberhalb von Crans-Montana.

Le glacier de Plaine-Morte, au-dessus de Crans-Montana.

The Plaine-Morte glacier above Crans-Montana.

*Der **Grosse St. Bernhard** bindet das Wallis mit der lienischen Aostatal. Im H auf der Passhöhe züchte Augustiner Mönche berühmten Bernhardine de.*

*Le **Grand-St-Bernard** re Valais à l'a vallée d'Aost Italie. A l'hospice situé s col, les moines augustins l'élevage des fameux c saint-bernard.*

...enorme distesa della Plaine orte...

El glaciar Plaine-Morte por encima de Crans-Montana.

Die typischen Holzhäuser von **Evolène** im Val d'Hérens.

Les chalets typiques d'**Evolène**, dans le val d'Hérens.

Typical wooden houses at **Evolène** in the Val d'Hérens.

▼

Le tipiche costruzioni in legno di **Evolène** nella val d'Hérens.

Las típicas casas de madera de **Evolène** en Val d'Hèrens.

Crans-Montana

The **Great Saint Bernard** connects the Valais with the Val d'Aosta in Italy. The Augustine Monks who inhabit the Hospice at the top of the pass breed the famous Saint-Bernard dogs.

Il passo del **Gran S. Bernardo** congiunge il Vallese con la Val d'Aosta-Italia. I monaci Agostiniani dell'Ospizio allevano il famoso cane S. Bernardo.

El **Gran San Bernardo** enlaza el país de Vaud con la Valle de Aosta italiano. En el hospicio, que se encuentra en el punto más alto del puerto de carretera, es donde los monjes agustinos crían los famosos perros San Bernardo.

Das 4478 m hohe **Matterhorn** mit seiner charakteristischen Pyramidenform ist eines der bekanntesten Wahrzeichen der Schweiz. Im Sommer wie im Winter zieht dieser Berg von einzigartiger Schönheit und Majestät unzählige Naturliebhaber an

Le **Cervin**, sommet de 4478 m caractérisé par sa forme pyramidale, est certainement une des images les plus connues de Suisse. Eté comme hiver, sa beauté majestueuse attire un grand nombre d'amis de la nature.

The **Matterhorn**, that characteristic pyramid rising to over 14,550 feet is one of the most famous Swiss landmarks. In Summer, as in Winter, this mountain of extraordinary beauty and majesty, draws countless nature lovers.

Il **Cervino** (m. 4478) dalla caratteristica forma a piramide, è il simbolo della Svizzera, un monte unico per imponenza e bellezza, meta di appassionati della natura sia in estate che in inverno.

El **Cervino**, de 4478 m de altitud, con su forma piramidal caracteristica, es uno de los simbolos más famosos de Suiza. Tanto en verano como en invierno, esta montaña de belleza y majestad realmente excepcionales es un punto de atracción de innumerables amantes de la naturaleza.

Zermatt, am Fusse des Matterhorns, ist ein weltberühmter Ferienort, Ausgangspunkt für zahllose Touren und Wanderungen in die umliegende Bergwelt.

Zermatt, située au pied du Cervin, est un lieu de vacances mondialement réputé, point de départ d'une infinité de courses et de randonnées dans les montagnes avoisinantes.

Zermatt, at the foot of the Matterhorn, is a world-famous holiday resort and a base from which all manner of tours and hikes into the surrounding mountainside depart.

Zermatt, ai piedi del Cervino, è un famosissimo luogo di villeggiatura e base per innumerevoli escursioni sui monti tutti intorno.

Zermatt, al pie del Cervino, es el centro de vacaciones más conocido, punto de partida para innumerables excursiones y paseos en el mundo montañoso de los alrededores.

4634 m hoch ist die **Dufourspitze**, der höchste Gipfel des **Monte Rosa-Massivs.**

La Pointe Dufour, avec 4634 m d'altitude, est le sommet le plus élevé du massif du **Mont Rose.**

The **Dufour Peak**, the highest point of the **Monte Rosa** massif rises to over 15,060 feet.

Nel massiccio del **Monte Rosa** la cima più alta è di m. 4634.

La cresta del monte **Dufour** se encuentra a una altitud de 4634 m, y es la más alta del macizo del **Monte Rosa.**

Eine Zahnradbahn führt auf den **Gornergrat,** von wo man einen einzigartigen Ausblick auf das Matterhorn und den Monte Rosa geniesst.

Un chemin de fer à crémaillère monte au **Gornergrat,** d'où l'on jouit d'une vue exceptionnelle sur le Cervin et le Mont Rose.

A rack-railway takes you to the top of the **Gornergrat,** from where you can enjoy a unique view of the Matterhorn and Monte Rosa.

Una ferrovia a cremagliera conduce sulla cresta del **Gornergrat,** da cui si ha un magnifico panorama sul Cervino e sul Monte Rosa.

Un ferrocarril de cremallera permite el acceso a **Gornergrat,** desde donde se puede gozar de una impresionante vista sobre el Cervino y el Monte Rosa.

Saas Fee auf 1800 m Höhe ist ein bekannter Sommer–
und Wintersportort am Ende der berühmten Skipiste
«Haute Route».

Saas Fee est une station de sports d'été et d'hiver
connue, située à 1800 m d'altitude. Y aboutit la fameuse piste de ski «Haute route».

Saas-Fee, situated at an altitude of 5850 feet, is a
well-known Summer and Winter sports resort at the
end of the famous «Haute Route» ski run.

Saas-Fee, situata a m. 1800 d'altezza, è una importante località di sport invernali dove termina il famoso
percorso sciistico di alta montagna chiamato «Haute
Route».

Saas Fee, a 1800 m de altitud, es un conocido centro
deportivo de verano e invierno que se encuentra situado al final de la conocida pista de esqui «Haute
Route».

Eine Fahrt über die drei Pässe S
Furka und *Grimsel* ist eine der sch
Touren im Gebiet der Schweizer Alp
führt duch eine unberührte Natu
grossartigen Ausblicken. Sehensw
auch der Rhonegletscher und der
scher, der den Grimselstausee spei

La tournée des trois cols *Susten*, *Fu
Grimsel reste une des plus belles
sions dans les Alpes suisses. Elle c
au travers d'une nature intacte et off
points de vue splendides. Le glac
Rhône vaut également le déplaceme
même que le glacier alimentant le lac
ciel du Grimsel.

A trip over the three passes – the S
Furka and *Grimsel* – is one of the
beautiful trips that you can take
Swiss Alpine region. It takes you t
unspoiled nature and offers some sp
views. The Rhone Glacier and the
that feeds the Grimsel reservoir ar
worth a visit.

ro dei tre passi – **Susten**, **Furka**, **Grim-**
— è uno dei più attraenti nella regione
e Alpi Centrali, con meravigliosi pano-
i ed una natura intatta. Di grande inte-
se sono il ghiacciaio del Rodano e
llo che alimenta il lago artificiale di
nsel.

viaje a través de los tres puertos de
retera **Susten**, **Furka** y **Grimsel** consti-
e una de las excursiones más inolvida-
s en la región de los Alpes suizos.
duce a través de una naturaleza virgen
vistas maravillosas. Es igualmente
no de mención el glaciar del Ródano, y
bién el glaciar que alimenta el embalse
Grimsel.

Der sagenumwobene **St. Gotthard** ist von alters her das entscheidende Bindeglied zwischen Nord– und Südeuropa. Am Gotthardmassiv, dessen höchste Spitze eine Höhe von 3192 m erreicht, entspringt die Reuss. Die Passtrasse steigt bis auf 2114 m ü.M. Dort befindet sich das jahrhundertealte Hospiz.

Le **St-Gothard**, cadre d'actions légendaires, est, depuis les temps les plus reculés, le trait d'union déterminant entre le Nord et le Sud de l'Europe. La Reuss prend sa source dans le massif du Gothard, dont la pointe la plus élevée atteint 3192 m. La route du col monte jusqu'à 2114 m; au sommet se trouve l'hospice plusieurs fois centenaire.

The **St. Gotthard**, steeped in legend, has from the very earliest times been the decisive link between Northern and Southern Europe. The Gotthard Mountains, the highest peak of which rises to 10,374 feet, cradle the source of the River Reuss. The pass road climbs to 6871 feet above sea level to where the centuries old Hospice nestles.

Il mitico **S. Gottardo** fin dai tempi antichi è il punto di comunicazione cruciale fra il Nord Europa ed il Sud. Dal suo massiccio, la cui vetta più alta si innalza a m. 3192, hanno origine il Rodano, la Reuss, il Reno. Il passo stradale è a m. 2114. Vi si trovano un osservatorio ed un antichissimo ospizio.

El legendario **San Gotardo** ha sido desde hace mucho tiempo el elemento de enlace decisivo entre el norte y el sur de Europa. El rio Reuss nace en el macizo del Gotardo, cuya cumbre más alta tiene una altitud de 3192 m. La carretera sube hasta una altitud de 2114 m sobre el nivel del mar, siendo en este lugar, donde se encuentra el hospicio que se construyó hace más de un siglo.

St. Gotthard

Der **Nufenenpass,** an dem der Fluss Tessin entspringt, ist der kürzeste Verbindungsweg zwischen den Kantonen Tessin und Wallis. Vom 2478 m hohen Nufenen aus erstreckt sich der Gries-Gletscher, der einen Stausee speist.

Le col du **Nufenen,** où le Tessin prend sa source, est la liaison la plus courte entre les cantons du Tessin et du Valais. Du Nufenen, qui s'élève à 2478 m, s'étend le glacier du Gries, qui alimente un lac artificiel.

The **Nufenen Pass,** from where the River Ticino draws its source, is the shortest route between the cantons of Ticino and Valais. The Gries Glacier stretches down from the 8054 foot-high Nufenen to feed a reservoir.

Il **Passo di Novena**, sulle cui cime nasce il fiume Ticino, è la via di collegamento più breve tra il cantone omonimo ed il Vallese. Dal Monte Nufenen, altezza m. 2478, scende il ghiacciaio Gries, il quale alimenta direttamente un lago artificiale.

El **puerto de carretera Nufenen,** en el que nace el río Tesino, es la vía de enlace más corta entre los cantones Tesino y Vaud. Desde la parte más alta del puerto de Nufenen, situada a 2478 m de altitud, se extiende majestuosamente el glaciar Gries, que alimenta un embalse.

Airolo

Bellinzona ist die Hauptstadt des Kantons Tessin. Die drei mächtigen turmbewehrten Schlösser zeugen von seiner bewegten Vergangenheit.

Bellinzone est le chef-lieu du canton du Tessin. Trois châteaux solidement implantés et flanqués de tours témoignent d'un passé agité.

Bellinzona is the capital of the canton of Ticino. The three mighty castles with their towering defences bear witness to its troubled past.

Bellinzona è il capoluogo del Canton Ticino. I tre castelli turriti testimoniano il suo interessante passato.

Bellinzona es la capital del cantón Tesino. Los tres imponentes castillos, con sus torres, son clara prueba de su agitado pasado.

Ronco, **Ascona**, **Brissago** und **Locarno** sind vier bezaubernde Ortschaften am Ufer des Langensees.

Ronco, **Ascona**, **Brissago** et **Locarno** sont quatre localités enchanteresses situées sur les rives du lac Majeur.

Ronco, **Ascona**, **Brissago** and **Locarno** are four delightful villages along the banks of Lake Maggiore.

Ronco, **Ascona** e **Bris** **Locarno** sono altrettant cantevoli località sul Maggiore.

Ronco, Ascona, Brissago y *Locarno* son cuatro lugares encantadores situados a orillas del Lago de Lugano.

Das milde, sonnige Klima seines Sees macht **Lugano** zur Perle des Tessins. Wegen seiner üppigen, subtropischen Vegetation wird es zu Recht als «Garten» der Schweiz bezeichnet.

Grâce au climat doux et ensoleillé de son lac, **Lugano** est la perle du Tessin. Sa végétation subtropicale luxuriante la fait nommer à juste titre le «jardin de la Suisse».

The mild, sunny climate of the Lake of **Lugano** make the city of that name the pearl of the Ticino. Its lush, subtropical vegetation has justly earned it the title of «Garden» of Switzerland.

Privilegiata dal mite e dolce clima mediterraneo del lago, **Lugano** è la perla del Ticino. Per la sua rigogliosa vegetazione sub-tropicale, è il vero «giardino» della Svizzera.

El clima suave y soleado de su lago hace de **Lugano** la perla del Tesino. Su abundante vegetación subtropical explica que sea designada como el «jardin» de Suiza.

San Bernardino
Stausee
Bassin de retenue
Storage lake
Lago artificiale
Agua Artificial

VIA MALA

Chur ist die Hauptstadt des Kantons Graubünden, in dem zum Teil rätoromanisch, die vierte Landessprache, gesprochen wird. Graubünden bezeichnet man auch als das Land der tausend Täler. Hier, in einer intakten Natur von bezaubernder Schönheit, beginnen der Rhein und der Inn ihren Lauf.

Coire est le chef-lieu du canton des Grisons, canton où s'utilise partiellement le romanche, quatrième langue nationale. Les Grisons sont également nommés «Pays des mille vallées». C'est dans cette région, gratifiée d'une nature splendide restée intácte, que naissent le Rhin et l'Inn.

Chur is the capital of the canton of Graubünden in part of which Romansch, the fourth Swiss national language, is spoken. Graubünden is known as the land of the thousand valleys. Here, where Nature remains unspoilt, the Rivers Rhine and Inn begin their respective courses.

Coira è la capitale del Cantone dei Grigioni il quale ha una propria lingua, chiamata «ladino» o «romancio». I Grigioni sono il paese delle mille valli, in esso nascono i fiumi Reno ed Inn, in una natura intatta ed affascinante.

Coira es la capital del cantón de los Grisones donde se habla en parte el romanche, que es el cuarto idioma nacional. El cantón de los Grisones se caracteriza igualmente como el país de los mil valles. Aquí, en una naturaleza intacta de fascinante belleza, es donde inician su recorrido el Rin y el Inn.

Arosa und **Davos** sind berühmte Ferienorte Graubündens. Ebenso schön sind aber auch die weniger bekannten Orte, wahre Ferienparadiese, die im Sommer wie im Winter Gäste aus aller Welt anziehen.

Arosa et **Davos** sont des lieux de vacances réputés des Grisons. Mais des lieux paradisiaques moins connus attirent également, été comme hiver, des hôtes venant du monde entier.

Arosa and **Davos** are famous holiday resorts in the Graubunden. The less well-known but equally beautiful villages, each a true holiday paradise, draw visitors from all over the world in Summer and Winter alike.

Arosa e **Davos** sono i centri di cura e soggiorno più famosi del Cantone dei Grigioni, ma anche altre località meno conosciute sono altrettanto belle e piacevoli, vero paradiso di vacanze sia estive che invernali per un pubblico internazionale.

Arosa y **Davos** son dos famosos centros de vacaciones de los Grisones. Ahora bien, son igualmente bellos los lugares menos conocidos, verdaderos paraisos de vacaciones que atraen visitantes de todo el mundo, tanto en verano como en invierno.

Davos

Arosa

Davos

Der **Marmorerasee** liegt an der Strasse zum **J[u]pass,** welcher das Engadin mit dem übrigen Bünd[ner]land verbindet und ganzjährig befahrbar ist.

Le lac de **Marmorera** se trouve sur la route du **J[ulier]** ouverte toute l'année, qui relie l'Engadine avec le [reste] des Grisons.

The **Lake of Marmora** borders the road up to the **J[ulier] Pass** which connects the Engadine with the rest o[f the] canton and which is practicable the year round.

Il lago di **Marmorera** è sulla strada del **Passo Giu[lia] il** quale collega tra loro i Grigioni e l'Engadina.

El **lago Marmorea** se encuentra en la carretera qu[e sube] al puerto de **Julier,** el cual enlaza la region de [En]dina con el resto de la región de los Grisones, y [que] permite la circulación durante todo el año.

Im Sommer wie im Winter wird der beliebte Ferienort **St. Moritz** von einer illusteren Gästeschar aus der ganzen Welt besucht.

Eté comme hiver, **St-Moritz**, lieu de vacances favori, est gagnée par une foule d'hôtes illustres venus du monde entier.

In Summer as in Winter, the favourite holiday resort of **St. Moritz** is frequented by cohorts of illustrious visitors from the world over.

St. Moritz è una delle più rinomate stazioni turistiche del mondo, sia in inverno che in estate.

El muy apreciado centro de vacaciones **St. Moritz** es muy concurrido por los innumerables e ilustres visitantes de todo el mundo, tanto en verano como en invierno.

Berninagruppe

Tiefencastel, Touristenzentrum in malerischer Lage am Kreuzungspunkt der Julier–, Albula–, Schyn– und Lenzerheidestrassen.

Tiefencastel, centre touristique situé dans un cadre pittoresque, au croisement des routes du Julier, de l'Albula, du Schyn et de Lenzerheide.

Tiefencastel is a tourist centre in a picturesque setting where the Julier, Albula, Schyn and Lenzerheide roads meet.

Sulla strada del passo Giulia si incontra **Tiefencastel**, amena località a m. 884.

Tiefencastel, centro turistico situado en un lugar pintoresco en el punto donde se cruzan las carreteras Julier, Albula, Schyn y Lenzerheide.

Die Einfachheit und Charakterstärke der einheimischen Bevölkerung spiegeln sich im Dorfbild wieder. **Zuoz, Samedan, Celerina** und **Pontresina** sind Oasen des Friedens, in denen man ruhige und erholsame Ferien verbringen kann.

La simplicité et la force de caractère des autochtones se reflète dans la physionomie des villages. **Zuoz, Samedan, Celerina** et **Pontresina** sont des oasis de paix, idéales pour des vacances reposantes.

The simplicity and strength of character of the native population is reflected in the appearance of the villages. **Zuoz, Samedan, Celerina** and **Pontresina** are oases of peace which offer a calm and invigorating holiday setting.

La semplicità ed il carattere degli abitanti si riflettono nell'architettura del paese. **Zuoz, Samedan, Celerina, Pontresina** sono altrettanti oasi di serenità dove si possono trascorrere vacanze tranquille e rivitalizzanti.

La sencillez y la fortaleza de carácter de la población local se reflejan en la imagen del lugar. **Zuoz, Samedan, Celerina** y **Pontresina** son oasis de paz en los que es posible pasar unas vacaciones tranquilas y relajantes.

Die fröhlich verzierten Fenster sprechen von der Herzlichkeit und Gastlichkeit der Bündner.

Les fenêtres aux décorations plaisantes témoignent de la nature cordiale et accueillante des habitants.

The merrily decorated windows express the warm-heartedness and hospitality of the local people.

Le finestre decorate allegramente sembrano voler testimoniare l'ospitalità e la cordialità dei Grigionesi.

Las ventanas, alegremente adornadas, hablan de la cordialidad y hospitalidad de los habitantes de los Grisones.

Oberengadiner Seen, Piz della Margna

Die Gemse ist die Königin der Felsen und unzugänglichen Gipfelpfade.

Le chamois est le roi des rochers et des sentiers sommitaux inaccessibles.

The Gemse is the king of rocks and inaccessible mountains tracks.

Il camoscio, re delle rocce e dei sentieri inaccessibili delle vette.

La gamuza es el rey de las rocas y de senderos de picos inaccesibles.

Ghost
Gold

FIFTY-ODD BOOKS

BY

OREN ARNOLD

including these lost treasure stories
Hidden Treasure in the Wild West
Irons in the Fire

Ghost

Gold

by

OREN ARNOLD

The Naylor Company
Book Publishers of the Southwest
San Antonio, Texas

4th Edition — 1961

Enlarged and Revised — 1967

Preface

True?

Of course these stories are true! For what is truth if not unselfish hope, romance and inspiration? What good is truth if it be matter-of-factual and drab? Richest gold lies not in the mountains but in hearts of men. The fascination of lost gold is not in the finding or even the searching, but in the meditating, the daydreaming, the telling.

Thanks forever, then, to the friends who have gone with me into the wild free hills, and to the countless old timers, prospectors, miners, cowboys, Indians, Mexicans, hunters and happy outdoorsmen in whose hearts this incomparable legend holds sway. Many versions of this Superstition Mountain lost gold history have been told, many "proofs" presented for this and that. None of them can stand close scrutiny or has full documentation. I have set down the version most loved, most often heard around campfires. No other legend has so gripped the imagination of our people, partly because most of it definitely is true, and all of it is fascinating.

In 1934 a few dozen copies of the legend were published by The Dons Club of Phoenix, as souvenirs for a meeting. Suddenly there was brisk demand, and those copies now are high-priced items for collectors, when they can be found at all. Sustained interest prompted a revised, more-detailed version illustrated with photographs, for everyone to enjoy. By 1960 three large editions of this version had been published. Since then the legend has continued to grow, with new and often tragic developments added every few months. The memory of the old Dutchman simply wouldn't lie still!

Therefore, this fourth edition of the book is enlarged again, brought right up to date. No story in all America is more fascinating to our people than this ongoing, ageless one about ghost gold.

Oren Arnold

Warning!

The Lost Dutchman Mine in Superstition Mountain has lured dozens of men and women to destruction; hence our readers are warned not to go searching without adequate armed protection and guides. Report your plans to the sheriff's office nearest your point of entry, with definite date of your expected return. No handful of shining nuggets is worth a human life, and strange disaster has stalked many in that awesome mountain. Beware!

Contents

Picture Section between pages   56 and 57

List of Illustrations   x

1. For Love of Rosita Maria   11
2. The Wrath of Don Miguel   16
3. "Mountain of Gold"   22
4. Massacre!   30
5. "Old Snow Beard," the Dutchman   37
6. Cupidity and Conflict   45
7. "Not Far From Weaver's Needle"   53
8. The Skull of Adolf Ruth   57
9. Other Men's Lives   63
10. Modern Dramas in the Mountain   69
11. The Thunder Gods   75
12. Maps of the Lost Mine   78

List of Illustrations

PAGE

1 Bronze plaque on monument to prospector for whom mine is named, at the foot of Superstition Mountain.

2 Monument to Jacob Walz, "Snow Beard the Dutch-man."
Dudette prospector coming out of the Mountain.

3 Typical "map" sold to credulous mine-seekers.
Searching party at entrance to Geronimo's Cave.

4 Typical terrain at base of the Mountain.
Modern "Dons" with Superstition in background.

5 Sheriff Walter Laveen and W.A. Barkley guide.
Nugget and cuff-links of Dutchman.
Brownie Holmes searched for years.

6 Frederick Rawson, mine authority.
Mrs. Sina Lewis, lady prospector.
Weaver's Needle (El Sombrero).
"Tex" Barkley, mountain guide.

7 Typical prospectors, with V.S. Irwin, right.
Spanish spur, stirrup and bayonet from Superstition.

8 Baying of hound led to finding of Adolf Ruth's skull.
Bullet hole in Ruth's skull.
Adolf Ruth.

1. For Love of Rosita Maria

CARLOS was a handsome fellow, handsome and young. A little darker than usual, perhaps, and a little sullen at times. Silent and sullen, and very, very jealous. But that, said Rosita Maria, made him all the more charming.

He was not so shallow and obvious as the others. They — why they, at the mere flicker of an eyelash, were wanting to have the full measure of love's enjoyment. Carlos, though, was more distant. At the autumn fiesta he had danced twice with her, gallant and formal and of grace itself. But he had spoken few words. Rosita decided sagaciously that he would require a different treatment; she would, therefore, be haughty and cold, even while her lips were carefully provocative. For you, Señor Carlos, a snap of the fingers and a disdainful "pouff!"

Love, you must understand, was a serious enterprise in those romantic years in old Sonora. In the 1840's, a cattle ranch in Mexico must perforce be a business and a social entity in itself, and the fine art of wooing received as much studied attention as the sterner one of raising cattle. Don Miguel Peralta, Rosita's father, was himself a master at both. He, too, could woo!

The old women of the hacienda — the Peralta rancho really amounted to a little village clustered about the main house and patio, with its tiny mission there — declared, for instance, that gallant young Carlos was ill-born, the son of Don Miguel by a pretty chambermaid whom he had "adopted" into his household. If Rosita knew this she didn't care! Love was not finicky and meticulous in old Mexico: love was just

12

pleasurable — ah, lilting and laughing and sometimes dangerous, too!

Delicious little vixen that she was, Rosita made slaves of every male creature who visited her father's patio. She had a trick of nestling her scented hair and forehead right over a man's heart when he was a few years older than she, of slipping her face under his bolero and fingering its braid, while pretending to cry in childish fashion because the nice man was going away. No man could thus refuse to hold her, to comfort her with soft, caressing words. It had never occurred to papa Miguel that Rosita was now a grown young woman. When he eventually did discover that her charms were more than juvenile, he did so in a most exciting manner.

One moonlit evening near the hour of midnight, the watchman atop the ranchhouse tower sat up suddenly alert and peered out into the semi-darkness.

"BONG! BONG!" He quickly reached back and struck his gong.

The noise it made was violent — an alarm that instantly aroused every human being in the village.

In just a few seconds men came pouring out of their huts and houses, strapping on belts of ammunition, loading and clicking their rifles as they ran. Don Miguel himself, a sabre in hand and fully dressed, dashed from his bed chamber into the patio, where a vassal held his charger saddled and stamping to go. But when someone opened the patio gate —

"Rosita! My daughter!"

He drew back in amazement.

As if a hand had been raised for prayer, an abrupt hush settled over the assembled soldiers, the hubbub and bustle of quick mobilization silenced by this incredible vision there in the moonlight.

The tower watchman had not, as might have been expected, seen a band of hostile Indians approaching. His keen eyes had beheld no threatening cavalcade of peon thieves. Thieves did come from time to time; once they swooped down onto women busy at the river laundry, lassoed and carried away three young girls. But no such ominous danger confronted the watchman now.

From the shadows of the willow trees that lined the stream bank, down near the horse cor-

14

ral outside the gardens, he had however seen a lovely maiden running. Running and screaming and obviously very much distraught.

And — *Madre de Dios!* — she was entirely nude!

What the watchman almost failed to see, during the excitement of Don Miguel's greeting to Rosita at the patio entrance, was a man hastily lead a horse from the corral, mount it and dash away.

But in a few seconds all the villagers were standing agape, staring at the horseman and listening to the clatter of hoofs as he galloped frantically off to the northward.

2. The Wrath of Don Miguel

LOVE is indeed an unfathomable thing. Rosita sobbed out that Carlos had "attacked" her. Maybe he had; a virile man's strength may be profound against another man, but when a dark-haired girl with lips of carmine begins to taunt and tantalize — ah me! Oh, to be sure, there are arguments. Why did Carlos allow himself to face such temptation? Or why, indeed, was she outside unchaperoned? No matter, now. That romance is ended and

16

history crashes on, unwilling to pause for speculation on one lovers' quarrel.

Don Miguel Peralta, though, was flushed with anger.

Absolute ruler, almost, of a cattle kingdom there in Sonora, Don Miguel virtually held the prosperity and happiness, even the very lives, of 500-odd people in his hands. A picturesque gentleman was he. Spanish grandee of dignified mien, prone to selfishness and lusts, lover of pomp and ceremony and luxury and show. Two pistols he carried, and a dagger, too. Men he had beheaded with his gleaming sabre; others he had tortured when they got in his way. There in the patio he wrapped a robe about his lovely daughter until her women servants waddled up to care for her. Black, then, was the temper of him.

"Move, you dullards!" he roared at his assembled henchmen, his regiment of vaqueros now turned military men. "Why are you idiotically staring? Begone! Bring him to me! With my own hands will I tear the vitals from him, the god-forgotten swine!"

No matter if Carlos was or wasn't Don Miguel's own son. Punishment and revenge shrouded the patron's soul and reasoning — he yearned only to get his clutches onto the boy who had loved ardently and too well.

For a quarter hour the don roared and thundered, commanding men and threatening them, promising and warning and muttering, calling to God for a chance to confront the youth who had attacked his only (admitted) child. It was with much difficulty that the kindly priest of the ranch, Father Serrano, could make Don Miguel hearken to reasoning at all.

"It will be foolish, sire, to pursue Carlos without guides," the priest reminded him. "That region to the northward is a fester of murderous Indians. And trails after a short distance are not known. Carlos could not be tracked at night. Let us first bring men whose keen eyes can be trusted to follow him."

In the end the good padre's reasoning prevailed. Don Miguel sent messengers for an Indian acquaintance who lived with his villagers not far away, a man of known experience named Wolf's Nose.

With Wolf's Nose came one friend, also an Indian, and when the two of them learned what was wanted, they muttered their contempt.

18

"Humph!" scoffed Wolf's Nose. "Too many men, too many horses. Get lost. Take one man, two horses."

All of Don Miguel's threatening and arguing could not move him, and so in the end Wolf's Nose triumphed. He and his swarthy companion departed with light equipment, riding two of the fastest horses from the Peralta corrals. It was almost daybreak as the two Indian trailers rode out of the patio gates. Dawn had colored the horizon with a glint of Sonoran steel, bluing rapidly into morning hues, highlighting here and there a distant mountain peak and presaging the glory of brilliance soon to come. In the chill light not even Wolf's Nose could see horse's tracks, but he knew Carlos had headed for the northward, and he knew that the fleeing boy must of necessity go through Paso del Muerto — the Pass of Death. There, more than any other place, had Spaniards and their descendants been trapped by Indians in years gone by, and destiny still had its tragedies to record there. Beyond this gap in the mountains Wolf's Nose knew he could pick up a fleeing man's trail.

At breakfast time Don Miguel was still a

19

devil of anger. Rosita Maria by this time was patently enjoying the sensation she had created, and that added fire to her father's wrath. Yet he could not censure her; she of all persons was the one to whom he bowed. A cruel and exacting taskmaster to the hundreds of other men and women in his vassalage, he was himself slave to the beautiful daughter who was his own.

His anger, therefore, he vented on everyone else around him. The shuffling old woman who brought him his morning liquor received a kick on her spacious rump for her solicitations. The boy who tended him was soundly slapped for not hastening in strapping on his spurs.

By noon he had caused the erection of a scaffold in the patio, a high post with a cross bar and a pulley hanging from it. A rope through the pulley had a basket on one end.

"Oh, will you hang Carlos, padre mio?" Rosita cried.

Don Miguel glared at her. Then he explained.

"His despicable feet will be tied to the floor. The loose end of the rope will I tie to his hands. Rocks will be put in the basket. Each hour an-

20

other will be added. In two days, something, doubtless, will break!"

Word was passed in subdued whispers among the young men of the rancho and the village that it would be unwise hereafter to taste the lusciousness of the daughter of Don Miguel.

3. "Mountain of Gold"

TIME, so the savants tell us, assuages all anger, all pain. Particular credence must be given to the axiom if you have lived in old Mexico, for there, as nowhere else, yesterday is yesterday and today is today, with tomorrow scarcely a consideration.

It was so in the romantic episode of Carlos and Rosita.

Don Miguel stormed and stormed, and by the end of the week had stormed himself out. So, too, had the interest — direct and casual — of the rancho at large subsided. Cowboys and other workers quickly slipped back into their accustomed routines. Women and girls about the houses ceased mouthing of the scandal, for what, after all, is another pretty maiden and her man? By the second week even Don Miguel had resumed his afternoon siesta, and life on the expansive Peralta ranch went on much as before, Only — the ominous scaffold in the patio was allowed to stand.

The weeks passed into a month, and still there was no news of Carlos. No news in Sonora in the 1840's was very likely to be bad news. If, then, Carlos had met disaster, well and good. Disaster awaited him back at home anyway. Such mild interest as did crop out from time to time as the days passed languorously was not in Carlos but in the fate of Wolf's Nose and the man who trailed with him.

One mid-morning six weeks after the love tryst under the moonlight, the tower watchman again reached back and struck his gong.

As before, the men who were present quickly organized into a unit for military defense. Don Miguel appeared and demanded to know what the watchman had seen.

"It is an Indian, a runner!"

It was indeed a runner, and in a few moments the news spread that the runner was Wolf's Nose. A rider leading another horse was dispatched to meet him. Don Miguel and his followers waited in the cool shadows of the patio. Wolf's Nose was still breathing deeply when he dismounted and trotted in, holding a leathern pouch high.

He stopped before the master, panting, staring, eyes afire.

"Well, speak, you dog!" thundered the ranch owner. "Where is Carlos? Why have you come —"

Wolf's Nose extended the pouch, now opened.

"Look!" said he. "Look! LOOK!"

There before Don Miguel were a double handful of the richest golden nuggets human eyes had ever beheld.

The patron stared in amazement. Slowly he fingered the treasure.

One piece, as big as a walnut, appeared to be solid gold. Others were like gleaming marbles, only rough and odd of shape. A rock like an egg was streaked with yellow, veins of it as thick as a man's shoe sole.

Men and women crowded around the ranch

24

owner and the Indian, staring agape at this golden revelation. Then everybody demanded of Wolf's Nose where and when and how.

It was a day before he could tell them the whole story; an Indian is never very articulate, and Wolf's Nose was exhausted from many weary days on the trail. But by midnight every person in the village knew that, far to the northward, was a miraculous mountain of solid gold! It was more than just a rumor; the Indian guide who had pursued Carlos had come back with positive evidence, a bag of beautiful, inflaming proof!

Carlos the lover was dead, said Wolf's Nose.

For days the two Indians had pursued him. They had been always just a few hours behind. They had found many of his camps. They had found the carcass of a calf with only the choicest meat removed, where Carlos had taken food. They found a mutilated bisnaga, the thorny barrel cactus which, if cut into, will supply any traveler with two quarts or so of drinkable water. They found where Carlos had robbed the nests of the cactus wren, even where he had killed a rattlesnake and eaten its flesh which is, as a matter of fact, often very delicate and tasty.

Carlos of course had known that dire punishment awaited him if captured, and so he fled with that in mind. Always he pushed northward. Eventually he led his trailers across many miles of desert, skirting a river bank and finally tried to escape them by going into the slopes of a peculiarly awesome mountain.

It was in the fastnesses of this vast, jagged mountain that the two Indians at last encountered him, but not at all in the manner they had expected. Pausing for food and rest one night, Wolf's Nose and his friend were suddenly alarmed to see a horseman galloping toward them on the horizon. Instantly they saw that it was Carlos.

They grabbed their guns to be on guard and to arrest him, by death if need be.

"Do not shoot! I come back! I am here! I have gold!" The lad was shouting it, in half-hysterical fashion.

"Here is gold, much gold! And there is a mountain of it more!" He dismounted and exhibited his specimens to the excited Indians.

Wolf's Nose, red man that he was, had lived

long enough to recognize the value of this metal to white men. He knew, even as Carlos did, that with it any man could buy immunity from punishment, regardless of the crime.

The two red men went back with Carlos to the location of the ore treasure, and there indeed was the most dazzling bonanza human eyes had ever beheld.

It was far, far from home, high amid pinnacles and crags. It was in a country infested with enemy Indians who would never hesitate to kill. It was isolated from the Peralta ranch by many miles of drinkless desert, hundreds of varas of rock and sand. But, even so, it was a bonanza; man will conquer insuperable obstacles when he catches the scent of gold.

Carlos and the two trailers filled all their saddle bags with the precious ore. They found an old Indian olla or jug near the place, and filled it with nuggets too, concealing it because it was too heavy to carry. Then they marked well the mine's location and started back southward.

(The fact that the prehistoric pot had crumbling bones in it when found is truly symbolic. Normally such a vessel would have been regarded by the two Indians as sacred property of the ancient people, not to be disturbed; but men can change bones for gold without any qualms. Carlos wanted it as a private treasure, when he should return.)

As they rode away, shrewd Wolf's Nose pointed out to Carlos that the dominant landmark nearby was a high peak of reddish rock shaped exactly like the crown of some gigantic Mexican sombrero.

For almost a week they rode together, and at length came to the bank of a swollen stream. It was angry, muddy water, tearing through the desert land in paradoxical fashion. The desert, normally waterless, can have its torrents of rainfall on rare occasions. More often, though, the mountains — which always color the desert horizons — will collect sudden bounty from the Rain Gods and send down the dry washes a veritable wall of destructive silt-and-debris-laden water. It may all happen within half an hour, and then as quickly subside.

The three ore-bearing travelers encountered just such a swell, and impatience seized them. They elected, foolishly, to swim their horses across the stream. Churning, swirling eddies en-

28

gulfed them without mercy, and only Wolf's Nose, far luckier than he deserved, managed to escape by clinging to a floating cottonwood tree.

Downstream a mile next morning he found the stiff and bloated body of one of the horses wedged in among some brush and rocks. With his belt knife he cut off one of the bags of ore, then philosophically set out afoot on the long trek southward.

It was a hard trek indeed. Once he went two days and nights without a drop of water. A vicious cactus thorn caused him to limp for days. Enemy Indians saw him, and only by dint of much dodging did he get away. And hunger trekked with him every hour of his journey.

Such was the account of his adventures told when he returned to the ranchhouse patio that morning and exhibited his bag of gold. In no time at all every swarthy Latin in all Don Miguel's little Sonoran kingdom was willing to swear that the mysterious mountain far to the northward was one solid mass of gleaming yellow metal. Such is the delicious hysteria that accompanies gold fever.

4. Massacre!

THUS Carlos the lover was the first white man ever to see the rich treasure store in Superstition Mountain.

The mountain of course did not acquire its present very apt name for many years afterward, until American settlers came into the region and heard the local Indians' stories and histories of the place. But Don Miguel Peralta himself gave the first name to the mine that old Superstition holds. Remembering the landmark of rock that resembled the crown of a hat, he

called his bonanza La Mina Sombrera (The Hat Mine).

The folk tales about the immediate efforts to mine the rich ore are somewhat contradictory, but it seems very definite that Don Miguel sent in three mining expeditions before he sent the greatest one of all.

Immediately after Wolf's Nose returned with the news of the discovery, a caravan of about 50 horses and men, with Wolf's Nose again as the guide, started for Superstition Mountain and returned three weeks later with packs of ore worth many thousand pesos.

The men returning from this trip told that the mountain was not really a solid hill of gold, but the wealth that they brought back was still sufficient to offset any early exaggeration. You just can't be too exact and critical when you are staring at a fortune; your eyes bulge and your pulse leaps, and forthwith you go away to spread glad tidings of greedy joy.

Of the second expedition we know almost nothing, but it seems likely that Don Miguel could send only the fifty or so men that he sent in before. The reason was that he had the normal business of a cattleman to attend to, for a time. But after the confirming report and the ore evidence of the first expedition, he did begin at once to close out his livestock enterprise and devote his entire efforts to mining. Cows are bulky, awkward, unlovely things when compared to a nugget of gold, and no man wants to deal in both of them.

At about this juncture, news sifted down into Sonora that the United States of America and the government of Mexico had signed a treaty whereby the United States acquired all of that territory now known as Arizona, thus lopping off the northern part of Sonora wherein the mountain of La Mina Sombrera lay. Don Miguel heard the news with consternation. Americans would never recognize his ownership of the rich mine!

That was the Treaty of Guadalupe Hidalgo, in 1848, an agreement destined to change the course of western empire. Mexico doubtless laughed up her sleeve at the moment, thinking she had sloughed off to a gullible neighbor a parcel of land good only for sandstorms and murderous Indians. At the moment, Mexico was right. But the mine that Don Miguel Peralta held was just one crumb of the ultimate wealth to be taken from the vast region lost by that treaty.

Don Miguel took prompt action when he heard of the treaty.

"Tiburcio!" he called his lieutenant, "ten days from this morning we send four hundred picked men and every animal on the rancho to La Mina Sombrera to bring every possible bit of ore.

"Have the women and their helpers begin packing at once. We travel light, but we take a thousand mules to bring back gold. This will be the last expedition to the mine. Americans now own it."

Before the day was over all normal activity about the ranch had been suspended, and every effort was directed toward outfitting of a pack train. Excitement ran high. A share in the gold was promised to every family, and in anticipation wealth loomed large in the coffers of every home.

Picking the four hundred to go was not so easy. But in the end most of those who remained were old men or boys not yet grown.

One ambitious young fellow had just wed a particularly beautiful peon girl. Then abruptly he was eliminated from the list of those to go on the expedition.

Satiated momentarily with the loves of his Carmencita, the lad hastily but secretly sought audience with Don Miguel. With rare sagacity he appraised the character of the patron in whose vassalage he was.

"Master," he whispered to Don Miguel, "this girl I have married is beautiful! I who know can testify to her charm. But her will I give to you, if I may but go on the grand treasure expedition!"

So immeasurable was the importance attached to the last big trip into Superstition Mountain! So fanatical were the minds of men who yearned to go.

It was indeed almost the grandest epic of treasure hunting the western continent had ever known. You cannot blame romantic youths for being insane about it. You cannot blame Don Miguel himself for thinking that such an array of apparent strength as four hundred men and a thousand animals was immune from any Indian attack.

But he had issued orders to travel light, so that all possible ore could be brought back.

34

Speed, too, was essential. All together these things bred negligence and a false sense of security. This was enhanced when the miners actually reached the mountain, found the rich ore, loaded their animals and started on the slower but seemingly triumphant journey back home.

They had departed from the ranch patio one dawn amid the sounding trumpets and the cheers of women and men, gay banners flying and horses impatient to start. They had paused only for their priest's blessing, then had ridden dramatically away. Now they had finished their mining and soon would return home, where a welcome with far greater pomp and fanfare must surely await them. Excitement and good spirits among the Mexican expeditioners therefore ran high.

But alas, it has ever been at such moments that a grinning Fate steps in with malignant hand.

Apache Indians, bravest and fiercest warriors in all America, swooped down on the ore train as it emerged from the canyons of Superstition, attacked with such surprising ferocity that only the merest sham of defense could be offered.

The glory of the Peralta rancho was wiped out in one bloody half hour. Of the four hundred picked men, two escaped. Two boys, carried along as personal servants of Don Miguel.

Hysterical with fear, these two crawled under some bushes and so witnessed the massacre there on the side of the mountain, and by night slipped away from the shambles of blood and gore.

It was they who, months later, brought news of the disaster to the people down in Sonora. By sheer good fortune were they able to make the long, hazardous journey back home.

Each lad had an indelible mental impression of the mine's location. These two should, surely, have been warned by the death and danger seen on that fatal expedition. But with the passage of years, gold lure grows as sadness fades, always. Also, the boys could not have dreamed of encountering Jacob Walz, the Dutchman. That's where Fate slapped at them again, when they took a companion and — three brave but foolish treasure-seekers — started back to Superstition Mountain.

5· "Old Snow Beard," the Dutchman

JACOB WALZ (sometimes spelled Wolz) in time acquired the accurate nickname of "Old Snow Beard."

This powerful prospector was not so very old when he entered the drama of lost treasure in Superstition. He may have been 50 or 55. No matter. His beard was white, and bountiful. Not the fading, venerable gray of a grandfather, but the freakish, gleaming white that is ghostly and a little frightening. His was the more frightening because of the fierce eyes that

37

gleamed over it. Despite the physical similarity, Jacob Walz did not have the benign countenance of Santa Claus at all, but some peculiarly sagacious gentleman in a Phoenix saloon once said that the beard looked like the kind of grotesque mask the devil might wear.

Walz was a German, not a Hollander. Americans have carelessly made little distinction between the two nationalities, whereof Walz was known about the mining camps of Arizona and elsewhere as the Dutchman. "Old Snow Beard," the Dutchman. He was taciturn and cranky, and little children were by no means the only ones who feared him.

One day in the 1870's (exact dates now are not known) Walz set out alone, journeying from camp about where Roosevelt Dam now is located, to meet some men near the village of Florence. He expected to travel near the Salt River. But it occurred to him that he could make a short cut across Superstition Mountain and so save many miles.

He hadn't gone six miles from the river when an Indian's arrow streaked from ambush and nicked him, leaving a scar on his arm until his dying day.

Walz, brave and fearful himself, in that moment did just what you and I would do. He ducked and ran.

He ascertained that a wandering band of six Apaches had jumped him. No fool at all in the outdoors, he was able to fend them off, to prevent their surrounding him and catching him in a trap. Years later he said he thought three were killed by his bullets, but he wasn't sure. At any rate, when nightfall came he did a lot of plain and fancy crawling and caused them to lose his trail. In the darkness he walked several miles in order to be far away from them, but when daylight came again he was as lost as lost could be.

Moreover, in the excitement of escaping from the Indians he had lost all the water from his canteen. He felt sure that, by following the correct dry washes and canyons, he could go back to the river and get his bearings again, but he already was suffering from thirst and hunger. Superstition Mountain is not supplied with water in generous quantity, and Arizona's sunshine is very, very warm and very, very dry. By noon Jacob Walz was much alarmed at the new danger facing him. He was exhausted by the encounter with Indians and weakened by thirst.

Chance alone saved him.

He came unexpectedly upon a faint human trail and followed it. It led him near a dominant, oval-pointed landmark of rock, and as he abruptly rounded a knoll he found the camp of three Mexicans. They greeted him with cordiality but with much surprise.

"Water! Water!" he pleaded to them, and they hastened to supply him from their kegs. He drank greedily and then ate an enormous quantity of food. An hour later he had rested enough to regain his composure, so began to look about him.

"What in hellfire are you three greasers camped up here for?" Old Snow Beard demanded.

"Por el oro, señor. The gold. We get heem. The mine, eet ees ours."

"What gold? They ain't no gold in this country."

"Ah, si señor! Mucho oro! Eet ees La Mina Sombrera! Eet ees ours."

They made it clear that they had ownership of the mine, but they also naively boasted of the richness of it, even took old Jacob Walz to their nearby diggings and showed him the outcrop-

40

pings of ore and the rich veins in the quartz they were collecting.

Old Jake's eyes nearly popped out of his head, so amazed was he.

For ten years he had been in Arizona prospecting for gold or silver, and the best he had been able to do was a little sly high-grading from other miners. And yet, here before his eyes was the richest, most unbelievable bonanza of which man had ever dreamed!

He pretended complete ignorance of ores and mining, however, and so managed to inspect the property carefully. He fingered numerous bits of rock, his eyes gleaming at them, his breast heaving in sheer excitement. He asked the Mexicans every question he could think of that might elicit information valuable to him, and they in turn answered him in simple faith and hospitality. They had no way of knowing, of course, that a stench of cupidity was swelling in old Jacob Walz's brain, and surely they had no way of knowing that this stranger with the flowing white beard was a deadly shot with pistol or rifle. Likely, too, they figured themselves entirely safe by virtue of the fact that they were three to his one.

41

Jacob Walz had brought his rifle with him. The Mexicans' own guns were propped conveniently in their little lean-to shack, there by the side of a red-rock cliff. A pistol and a knife were in the Dutchman's belt.

Walz cautiously edged away from his hosts so that several feet separated him and them and he was nearest to their shack, just a step or two from his own rifle. Suddenly he spoke, as if alarmed.

"Ain't that some men a-coming yonder?" he demanded, pointing.

All three of the others turned away from him. Walz then calmly picked up his gun, stepped to one side so as to throw two of the Mexicans directly in line with him, lifted the rifle and fired.

The two men crumpled, the scream of one rending the air in horrible manner.

The third turned, saw Walz was about to kill him.

"NO! NO! In the name of —! "

A second shot quieted him too, forever.

For two minutes or more old Walz stared at the bodies, waiting to be sure all three men were dead.

Then he looked around a bit and eventually dragged all three of his victims about 150 yards to a deep and narrow cervasse in the side of the mountain, dumped them in it and piled rocks on top of them. Three brave lads, hearty adventurers, victims at last of that most pernicious malady of all, gold fever; murdered there in the mountain with no one, this time, to carry news of the tragedy back to Sonora. Having finished the burial, Walz went back to the mine, collected a double handful of the richest nuggets and squatted there staring at them and enjoying them for a long time.

This is the exact manner in which Jacob Walz, the Dutchman, acquired ownership of the rich gold mine in Superstition Mountain. He told those details himself some years later as he lay dying in his home in Phoenix, told them to a man named Dick Holmes, a reputable citizen who himself died as recently as 1930. He said that he had had no compunction about it, inasmuch as the mine owners were only "greasers" anyway. He also told of many more killings that he had done.

At this writing, many men and women still alive remember Jacob Walz well, and many facts are known about him; but the facts in this narrative are just those which he himself attested to. They are tragic enough, without any embellishment from his neighbors.

6. Cupidity and Conflict

OLD WALZ collected all the golden nuggets he could that day, came on out of the mountain to Phoenix and did a characteristic thing. He went over to a saloon and got rip-roaring drunk.

"Waugh! I'm a two-legged hellion rarin' to fight!" He shrilled it to all and sundry persons up and down what is now Washington Street. Nobody paid much attention to the old fool, but everybody kept out of his way. The drunker he got, the more he ranted and boasted.

"I got a private graveyard in th' mountain and I'll fill it up yet! Got enough gold to pave this street, and I'll blow hell outen any man that tries to steal it!"

This last boast commanded more attention.

A man is likely to talk unguardedly when fired with alcohol, and a boast of gold is dangerous any time. Moreover, old Jacob came into the Phoenix saloons with a bag of generous proof. He did indeed have gold, because he paid for things with it! Bartenders' eyes bulged at the nuggets he showed. Loafers plied him with questions, cautiously but thoroughly, but learned little of the location of his mine.

Therefore the inevitable happened. The old man was followed when he next set out for the mountain, heading for his rich bonanza.

He left Phoenix prodding three burros, taking a complete pack of tools and grub, not to mention a generous supply of guns and ammunition. He wouldn't tell where he was going, and he wouldn't say when he would be back. If he knew about his indiscretions of speech when intoxicated, he made no reference to them.

But he was no fool. The fourth night out,

he built his little campfire, ate supper and apparently took his blankets over into some scrubby bushes for a night of sleep.

About two hours later, however, some quick shots broke the still of evening, down the draw half a mile behind him.

If, at that moment, some investigator had looked into Jacob Walz's bed there in the bushes, the blankets but not the Dutchman would have been found. And it is a fact that some cowboys a few weeks later did find the remains of two well-known Phoenix men, not far from where Jacob Walz had been camping!

He did not always slip back and slay his followers. Oftentimes, so he told later, he wasn't "in the notion to do no killin' " (probably even the toughest of us have tender moods at times!) and so when he saw his followers, he just camped. He had a favorite campsite by a prehistoric Indian ruin, even cooked in some of the pots the ancients had used.

Just camped and waited. Or moved to the nearest stream and panned gold, picking up maybe a dollar or two a day, until eventually he wore out the patience of his followers. If he was in a big hurry he might back-track and dodge and so throw his shadows off the trail, for he was an expert at such practice, but in such cases it usually was easier to kill than to dodge.

Two soldiers one day made the same mistake that the three Mexicans from whom Walz stole the mine, had made.

They were army men who had also the duty of carrying the mail, and they were not averse to discovering any natural treasure that Arizona might afford. Like most of the men about this region at the time, they yearned to have a share of "Old Snow Beard's" bonanza.

They might have had, too, with a little more caution.

They outwitted Walz at first and did track him right to the location of his mine. Then, evidently fancying themselves safe from harm because they were two to one, they foolishly shouted at him and went running down the mountain slope, elated over being within sight of the rich treasure.

In a few seconds, however, they were dead.

Walz shot both of them. The body of one rolled, bump-thud-bump, down over the rocky incline to the murderer's very feet. The white-bearded old devil calmly tied a rope around their legs, hitched a burro to them and dragged them to that same crevasse into which he had dropped the Mexicans. He had, in all truth, a private graveyard there in the mountains.

A man named Phipps back-trailed the Dutchman one week, and so came onto his unbelieveably rich gold mine.

Phipps was beside himself with excitement. His first thought was to take all the treasure he could and run with it. Saner reasoning, however, told him that he could do more with a pack train and some help. With a man to aid him, he could readily come back, fight off the old hermit prospector if he should catch them, and so take a double fortune of the gold. This he elected to do.

He hastened to his home camp near the present town of Superior and went down into an old abandoned mine shaft to get a favorite pick. Nobody ever knew just what happened, but something caused the shaft to cave in, and Phipps was killed. He died without revealing to his friend where the Dutchman's mine was located.

"It's less'n two mile from Weaver's Needle,"

49

Phipps told, "and man she's a ring-tooter for money! I seen a fortune without swinging a pick."

Weaver's Needle was the new name given to that landmark first called The Hat. It suggested the crown of a Mexican sombrero, and also resembled the oval-pointed needle commonly used in weaving. The new name sticks to this day.

Another man, named Deering, also found Jacob Walz's Superstition Mountain mine. Deering eluded the Dutchman's watchful eye and murderous rifle, noted carefully the mine's location and, like Phipps, came out to get help in working it. He showed up at Florence all agog with excitment and plans, safe in the knowledge that with a few choice friends to help him, he could shovel out his million dollars and go back East once more.

But he passes out of the narrative right quickly also. He, too, got drunk. The drunker he got, the more he boasted. Soon a fellow tippler got enough of him and drove a Mexican dagger through Deering's heart. Old-timers now say that Deering was the seventh man to die, a direct victim of the gold spell cast by Superstition Mountain, not counting the lives lost when Don Miguel Peralta owned the mine.

One old-timer tells of seeing Walz have a gun battle with a big black-mustachioed sheriff. The sheriff fired six times, and Walz was only slightly injured, but the one time that the Dutchman fired netted the sheriff a month in bed.

Persistent efforts of his fellow men to find his treasure trove so enraged Jacob Walz that the old fellow decided he must have help. He trusted a few people, had only one or two friends. Clannish by nature, he therefore wrote back to Germany and asked his own nephew to come to Arizona and help him.

"I told Julius (the nephew) what a fine country it was," old Walz related on his deathbed. "I told him I had taken thousands of dollars from my mine, and asked him to come and help me. I knew he was living in poverty back at home. I even sent him money to come on."

And come Julius did! He could speak no English, but when, some months later, old Walz showed him the gold there in Superstition, Julius' flow of German exclamations must have been notable. Here indeed was wealth like few men in all Europe ever knew!

The uncle and nephew took out a burro-

51

load of the rich ore and headed back for Phoenix. All the way Julius was garrulous, full of plans for spending the money, dreaming audibly in the intoxication of free gold. Morose old Jacob began to tire of him.

At Phoenix young Julius became a spendthrift, and within a month the two had to head for their mountain "mint" again. Julius continued boasting. Boasting and bragging and swaggering and generally allowing his emotions to run off with his judgment. That was bad.

The two were encamped near the present town of Temple one night on that second journey, when old Walz again let cupidity get the best of him. Without warning he snatched up his rifle and put a bullet through his own nephew's brain.

Then he tied a length of chain round Julius' neck, dragged the body a few yards to a shallow grave in the sand under an overhanging lip of rock and buried it there.

Julius the nephew was number eight in the chain of deaths, due directly to the Dutchman's insane jealousy and greed.

7. "Not Far From Weaver's Needle"

BUT in time it also came Jacob Walz's turn to die.

The old man stayed in a shack down by the Salt River when he had barely enough money to live. An Indian squaw, called Old Red, was his woman there.

When he got rich from his Superstition mine, however, he took a blacksnake whip of the type mule skinners used and drove Old Red away.

Then he moved to Phoenix and "took up" with a woman said to be half Negro.

This new woman was a prettier and a younger one. She had "power." She could look a man in the eye and make him sing to her, and incidentally empty his pocketbook. She could, and did, build a little fire in her adobe apartment, throw some powders onto it and make queer colored smokes in which she said her spirits lived. With this impressive manifestation, she built up quite a little religious following in Phoenix at one time. Old Walz was one of her converts, physically as well as spiritually.

Wet in a storm one day, he soon lay ill of pneumonia. Obviously he was going to die. He sent the half-breed woman for the doctor, and she also encountered Dick Holmes.

"Mistuh Ho'mes, will you go ovah to our house?" she pleaded. "Old Dutchman, he 'bout to die."

Holmes went over and sat by the Dutchman's bed.

There it was that Jacob Walz related his entire story, from the killing of the three Mexicans to the murder of his own nephew. He told of them in detail, even mentioned the length of

54

chain with which he dragged his nephew to the grave. (Later Holmes went to the spot and exhumed the nephew's body, found the bullet hole in the forehead and the piece of chain around the neck. The boy's skull was exhibited for years in Temple by a physician.)

The dying Walz also tried to tell Holmes the location of his mine.

"You are the only man friendly enough to come to see me," Walz muttered. "Look under my bed, Holmes. Get the box you see there. What's in it is yours. There is a map to the mine, too. It will be good if you know the key.

"The key is a stripped palo verde tree with a pointing arm, one limb left on. It points away from Weaver's Needle, not toward it. About halfway between it and Weaver's Needle, and 200 yards to the east, is the richest gold mine I ever heard of.

"When I was up there the last time, I covered up the mine shaft.

"I put heavy ironwood logs acrost the opening, piled rocks and dirt on top of that. Then I planted a cactus on the spot, but it mightn't live. I scraped off all signs of camping. I didn't want nobody to steal it whilst I was gone.

"But the gold's still thar, not far from Weaver's Needle. You go get it for yourself. Goodby."

With that, Jacob Walz died. Dick Holmes spent twenty-eight years trying to find the property, and himself died a disappointed man. His wife still lives at this writing, and his sons still have hopes of locating the bonanza some day. None of them has ever located the palo verde with the pointing arm.

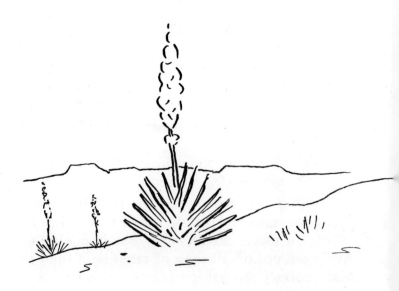

HERE LIE THE REMAINS OF

SNOWBEARD

THE

DUTCHMAN

WHO IN THIS MOUNTAIN SHOT THREE MEN TO STEAL A RICH GOLD MINE FROM SPANISH PIONEERS, KILLED EIGHT MORE TO HOLD HIS TREASURE, THEN HIMSELF DIED IN 1892, WITHOUT REVEALING ITS LOCATION. DOZENS OF SEARCHERS HAVE MET MYSTERIOUS DEATH IN THE CANYONS THERE, YET THE ORE LIES UNREVEALED. INDIANS SAY THIS IS THE CURSE OF THE THUNDER GODS ON WHITE MAN IN WHOM THE CRAVING FOR GOLD IS STRONG. BEWARE, LEST YOU TOO SUCCUMB TO THE LURE OF THE LOST DUTCH-MAN MINE IN SUPERSTITION MOUNTAIN. ERECTED BY

1938

Bronze plaque on monument to prospector for whom mine is named, at the foot of Superstition Mountain.

Monument to Jacob Walz, "Snow Beard the Dutchman."

Dudette prospector coming out of the Mountain.

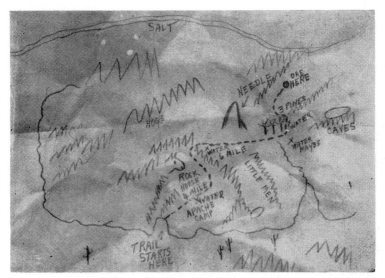

Typical "map" sold to credulous mine-seekers.

Searching party at entrance to Geronimo's Cave.

Modern "Dons" with Superstition in background.

Typical terrain at base of the Mountain.

Sheriff Walter Laveen and W. A. Barkley guide.

Nugget and cuff-links of Dutchman.

Brownie Holmes searched for years.

Frederick Rawson, mine authority.

Mrs. Sina Lewis, lady prospector.

Weaver's Needle (El Sombrero).

"Tex" Barkley, mountain guide.

Typical prospectors, with V. S. Irwin, right.

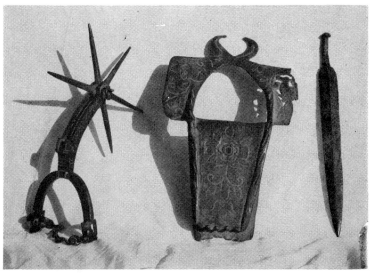

Spanish spur, stirrup and bayonet from Superstition.

Baying of hound led to finding of Adolf Ruth's skull.

Bullet hole in Ruth's skull.

Adolf Ruth.

8. The Skull of Adolf Ruth

OLD Jacob Walz, the Dutchman, was buried in the West Jefferson Street cemetery in Phoenix, but with his death the mine he stole took life anew. Since that day of his passing, half the population of Arizona has felt the urge to go searching for his property, and a surprising number of them have actually gone.

Not only is this the most famous mine in Arizona, but its fascination has spread to other states as well. By actual count, in one twelve-month period since 1930, one hundred and forty-six persons were known to have come to Arizona, to go hunting for Superstition's gold.

The one among them who created most sensation was Adolph Ruth.

Adolf's son, Dr. Erwin C. Ruth, had occasion to go Mexico on business and while there did some favors for descendants of old Don Miguel Peralta. He attached no importance to these favors, but he did show a scholar's interest in Mexican arts and crafts, historical papers, museum relics and such. The Peralta household was pleased to show him its heirlooms — including a quaint old map handed down for decades and purporting to locate a mine in a distant mountain. Dr. Ruth studied it at length.

"This is an interesting piece," he said to his hosts.

"You like it, señor?" one of them asked.

"Why — why, yes. The drawing, lettering — everything on it — makes it of interest, I think."

"It is yours. It is pleasure to make him a gift to you."

That's Mexican hospitality for you. It would

58

have been all the same if he had admired a horse or a chair. Moreover, courtesy forbade his declining the gift, having gone this far. He thanked them and in due time took the old map home. It had no intrinsic value, so far as he or his hosts knew. Just a funny old relic.

Dr. Ruth's home was in Washington, D. C., and he let the old map lie around there carelessly for some months, then one day chanced to show it to his father, a 66-year-old government employee. Adolf Ruth studied it a minute or two.

"Whe-euw!" the father breathed. "Where'd you get this, son?"

"Aw, it's nothing. Picked it up down in Mexico."

"It's valuable!"

"Bosh!"

"I say it is. I — I've been reading about the mine in Superstition Mountain. In Arizona. A lost treasure."

Dr. Ruth was amused. He had no interest in ghost gold. "Okay, Dad, the map's yours. I hope it makes you rich."

He spoke jokingly, but his father was intent. Within that week Adolf Ruth had resigned his job, pooled his assets, bought an old car and headed westward. He arrived in Phoenix in June, 1931.

Against all the advice of skilled outdoorsmen, who knew the hot, waterless nature of Superstition Mountain in summer, Mr. Ruth shouldered his pack and headed in. Two cowboys, Jack Keenan and L. F. Purnell, carried part of his provisions a short way into the mountain canyons and agreed to meet him again at this, his first campsite, at the end of thirty days.

But at the end of thirty days Mr. Ruth did not show up.

Six weeks passed and he still was not to be found.

Dr. Ruth, the son, was notified, and he came out from Washington to conduct a search. Officers with horses and dogs, even airplanes, were used in scouting over the awesome old mountain. Guns were fired, signal fires were lighted, smokes were made, the cliffs and canyons were surveyed as carefully as possible, but no trace of the lost prospector could be found.

Finally Dr. Ruth gave it up and went sadly on back home. Sheriff's officers told him that his father had not one chance in a million to be alive, because his supply of water and food must long since have been exhausted. Headlines that had been spread all over the front pages dropped then to inside small ones, and finally quit entirely as public interest turned elsewhere.

In December of that same year, however, a quite accidental discovery added another chapter to the mystery.

An archaeological party, headed by newspaper representatives and the Phoenix city archaeologist, formed a cavalacade into Superstition seeking prehistoric Indian ruins. A hound dog with them suddenly darted over to a palo verde tree and sniffed at something there on the ground.

"Old Spot's found something," one rider remarked.

"May be a rattler," said another. "Late for snakes, though."

"I'll ride over there."

Just mild curiosity prompted the move, but when the rider got near the dog, he called out again:

"Why, it's a human skull!"

They photographed it as it lay, then examined it. The scientist in the party said it was indubitably the skull of an elderly man. It must be Adolf Ruth's!

It was. Half a mile away, after much circling and hunting, they found Ruth's headless torso. Coyotes or other predatory animals had ravaged the body and carried the head away, but there, intact, was every item of his personal luggage — his blanket, his notebook, his flashlight, his canteen with a little water still in it, even his unfired pistol — save one thing. The map Mr. Ruth had carried was missing!

Ruth's skull had a hole through the left temple, unquestionably made by a bullet, scientists declared.

Moreover, definite suspicion was pointed at some men, but no proof of murder has been found to date, and Ruth's death is still a mystery.

It is a mystery, that is, so far as the cold records go. But to those of us who know the mountain's background of grim tragedy, it is no mystery at all. Somebody wanted that map and killed to get it. Old Superstition just claimed another life from the list of men who have sought to take away her gleaming gold.

9. Other Men's Lives

THE death of Adolf Ruth was the most sensational of recent tragedies in Superstition, but is by no means the sum of them.

In 1928 two deer hunters — not gold seekers at all — tackled the mountain and barely escaped with their lives when "somebody" started rolling huge stones down the mountainside. They never knew just who attacked them.

They were more fortunate than the father and two sons from New Jersey, who read of the Lost Dutchman Mine in Eastern newspapers and came out to hunt for it. The rocks that were rolled at them broke the leg of one boy and utterly demolished their camp and equipment so that they almost died of thirst before they could trek out of the mountain.

Calvin Blaine and Ray Schweiger, both reputable citizens of Phoenix, were hiking in Superstition in 1932 when some unknown assailant began shooting at them.

"We were about half way up the mountainside," says Mr. Blaine, "when we began to hear rifle shots in the distance, coming from across a canyon, and higher up.

"At first we thought it was just hunters, but then we noticed bullets going 'plop' around us!

"We quickly hid behind some rocks. All we had to answer with was a little .22 calibre rifle, useless at long range.

"The shooting stopped, but every time we peered out it started again. Once I held up my hat on the rifle, and two bullets were fired at it. We could hear them go zinging off the rocks when they struck nearby.

"It is foolish to say we were not frightened, but near nightfall we slipped out and got back to our car unharmed. We reported to the

64

sheriff, but he could not find who attacked us."

The skeleton of a woman was reported found in a cave up in Superstition a few years ago, but there was no clue to her identity.

The skeleton of a horse, a man's skull and arm bones, and an old rusted rifle were found there. Numerous rusted spurs, miners' picks, harness rings and such mementos have been picked up, obviously relics of Don Miguel Peralta's ill-fated expedition of decades ago.

Several people have gone gold-hunting into the mountain and never been heard of again. Whether they became lost and so perished there, or slipped out unobserved, nobody can say. Three Texas boys came to Arizona, wrote back from Phoenix that they were leaving in a few hours to find the lost mine. They were never heard of again.

V. S. Irwin, who lived for twenty years near the base of Superstition and often prospected there, exhibits signed documents stating he has sold valuable carloads of gold ore from the mountain, but in all his searching he has never found the richest treasure-lode of all — the Lost Dutchman.

A fellow named Williams, a resident of

Phoenix, went with his wife to the base of Superstition one winter day, on a picnic. The sky was sunny, and he decided to hike up a way alone, while she rested at their car. At sundown he had not returned. At nine o'clock he had not returned, and Mrs. Williams drove back to Apache Junction, about ten miles, for help.

Nothing could be done that night, and when dawn came a blizzard was snorting from the Four Peaks area to the northeast, driving rain and sleet and snow all over Superstition's canyons. Nevertheless, searchers went in. Officers organized posses with provisions for food and warmth. The missing man's American Legion post sent out a large contingent, and many other men volunteered. All told, about three hundred people engaged in that manhunt, without success.

When they had all but given up the search, due to storm and lack of clues, Williams himself staggered down out of the mountain.

"I huddled back in a cave," he explained, "and look here — !"

Even as Carlos had done, decades ago, Williams clutched gold! It was a peculiar form of

66

gold, in little sticks or sheets, thick like heavy pasteboard, not in nugget or ore form.

Williams was dirty and disheveled and hungry, and he declared he had sought refuge from the storm in the cave and there had found a pocket of gold. The sticks of it, said he, were all in a pile.

The gold was genuine. Some tried to say it was dental gold, stolen from a sanatorium by somebody and hidden there. Old timers, however, declared that it was in stick form because it was "concentrates." Spaniards or Mexicans, said these men, often smelted down their richest ore right there in the mountain, pouring their concentrated metal into little holes or depressions in rocks to cool and harden. This would save carrying waste weight back to Mexico on muleback. Obviously they would have stored it in caves until they were ready to go back to Mexico, and they might have overlooked some of it on their last trip, or left it there for future transportation.

William's experience created sensation anew, and he made yet another sortie into the mountain, so that his name in the headlines was a common sight in Arizona for a while. But people began to question his statements, some scoffing, some wanting to share his wealth. Wisely, he "laid low" until interest in him could subside. It may have been that he was closer to the hidden treasure than anyone else.

Another energetic young man came into Arizona about 1937 and conducted what he termed exhaustive search for the mine. He had an impressive assortment of maps, sketches and notes — enough to "almost" locate the hidden bonanza, it seems. Several people were impressed, but last heard of this prospector was when he sought to borrow a few dollars to go into the mountain once more. As always, it appeared that Superstition's gold was just over the next canyon wall somewhere.

The Dons Club of Phoenix, ambitious students of Southwestern legend and lore, grubstaked two men on a long searching expedition into Superstition. Their prospectors staked out a nice claim, right enough. But they could not locate the shaft that old Jacob Walz had covered with ironwood logs, rocks and soil.

10. Modern Dramas in the Mountain

MOST lost treasures tend to recede as time passes, moving back into the dim pages of history, forgotten except by the few who bother to read of doings in the olden days.

Not so, the Lost Dutchman!

That great bearded ghost was walking the canyons of Superstition Mountain right on through the 1940's, the 1950's, the 1960's. Doubtless it will be "alive" and active when Westerners celebrate the dawning of Century Number 21.

Since 1950 at least a dozen *more* lives have been sacrificed in the too-often frantic search for those mystery millions. The number may well be two or three times that, because other men and women have simply disappeared after entering the mountain, and while some may have come back out unannounced, many undoubtedly remain there now as bleaching bones.

Their true stories tend to follow a pattern of similarity.

"I read about the gold in a magazine," gushed one fuzzy-faced collegian from Pittsburgh. "I aim to stay in there until I find it."

"Don't go, son, don't go," pleaded the Pinal County sheriff. "By law I can't stop you. But I urge you to settle down out here somewhere, get a good job and *earn* a fortune. Hundreds of bright young fellows like you are doing just that. It's much safer."

"Who's afraid?" scoffed the boy, grinning.

He walked into the mountain canyons with a gallon of water, a pick, a pack of grub, and a train load of confidence. About 16 months later two hunters up there buried his buzzard-picked remains.

Ted Delaney and Buster Waldron were more

fortunate. They, too, were college boys, but on a vacation lark they went in together. Three days later Ted staggered out, his clothing ripped by briars and thorns, his hat gone and his face bubbled with sun blisters, but his mind was still clear.

"That very first night," he reported, "somebody started shooting at us. All we had was a pistol apiece, and not many bullets. We separated and shot back, but never really saw anybody. Buster twisted his knee running in the rocks. I've got him hidden now in the shade, but we have to go get him quick or he'll die."

They got him safely out with a helicopter lift.

Two 17-year-old boys from Minneapolis, Charles Skelton and Charles Matterson, almost duplicated that experience. They went into the mountain with a rifle and 70 rounds of ammunition. Skeldon limped out, and three days later a possee found Matterson four miles from water, "all in," with his pack and rifle lost. Both boys told of hearing mysterious voices in the mountain, but saw no other people despite their own calls.

Alan Jerome and Don De Yough from Long

Island, N. Y., hitchhiked to Arizona, hurried into Superstition Mountain, and have not been heard of in Arizona since. The local folk *hope* they got out safely.

Another modern "scientist" said that he had been using extra-sensory perception to locate the lost mine and knew exactly where it could be found. He seemed very sincere. He went in, grimly, confidently. Six months later he hadn't been heard from. Then a friend and fellow ESP expert tried to locate him by brain work. He too went into the mountain — and presumably is still there. Neither man has reported any findings, or indeed been heard of again.

Euselo Castelar, an educated geologist in Spain, somehow learned of treasure in the mystery mountain of far-away Arizona, and made his way out there. He is known to have searched for years, and even built himself a crude cabin near a dependable source of water. But on May 6, 1965, two other prospectors found Euselo's body, another sacrifice to the lust for gold.

One chap in 1965 may truly have had a bit of luck. He came out and reported that he had found "abundant gold."

72

"How much is 'abundant'?" a deputy sheriff asked.

"Well, I sold enough to have about $71,500 in cash," the man declared. A checkup showed that he had really sold a lot of ore.

"What became of the money?" they asked him.

"That's what hurts," the man said. "My wife was in there with me, but she got mighty restless. She drugged me and lit out, taking all that money. Now I can't find our diggings again, I was grieving so. Will you help me find her?"

Chalk up another and deeper tragedy for old Superstition. It is hard enough on a man to lose a fortune; it is even harder to lose a once-loved wife.

Still another searcher was wandering around up there, crazed from having drunk stagnant water. He was more fortunate than many; they found him in time to get him to a hospital and restore his health. But he left swearing to go back in "and find that Lost Dutchman Mine if it kills me." It probably will; perhaps already has.

On April 29, 1966, Glenn Magill and five

associates from Oklahoma City came out of the mountain saying they positively had located the lost mine, and backed their claim with a bag of rich gold nuggets. They said they used an old map obtained from a man who had made it in 1931, from a still older Mexican map.

Nobody openly accused them of anything, but few people took them seriously. The Lost Dutchman has been "found" dozens of times — by persons who then want to sell you a map, or want you to grubstake them to the tune of $100 or $1,000 or whatever you can afford. Mr. Magill and his party may be entirely honest, but by October, 1966 no grand excitement had developed, as it surely would have if the real Dutchman had been found.

Helicopter rescues nowadays make searching a bit safer. But too often the "chopper" has to bring out a corpse rather than a living soul.

"The old Dutchman Mine is still hidden up there," one authority vows. "If anybody ever finds *that,* he'll know it, and be able to prove it so forcefully that all of America will be excited.

"Meanwhile, about 2,000 people a year go in there searching."

11. The Thunder Gods

ALTHOUGH the name Superstition is English, of course, and was given to the mountain, very appropriately, by the early white settlers, the Indians of the vicinity had given it a similar name in their own language years before.

It happens that many a rainstorm originates in Superstition. On warm afternoons in spring, great masses of black clouds will gather up there, settling so low as to hide Weaver's Needle and similar peaks, then will come crashing down the valley in majestic noise and anger.

Hence it was inevitable that Indians regarded the place as the residence of the Thunder Gods, and many red men so regard it to this day.

Other Indian tales say that Superstition houses the counterpart of our devil, and that this satanic being lurks diabolically there to kill men who would steal his gold.

Still other Indian superstitions about the mountain arose from the fact that the Apache Trail skirts it. In the olden days, the fierce, predatory Apache Indians swooped down from that region and carried off the food and women of the agricultural Indians below. These Apaches, fiercest of all savages, capitalized on the fear that they thus instilled in the Pimas and Maricopas, and the latter in turn looked eastward to Superstition Mountain as the dwelling place of danger. To this day few Indians will actually go into the canyons and fastnesses of Superstition alone.

An army doctor stationed at Fort McDowell in the old days, so the story goes, helped an Indian village defeat contagious disease, thereby saving many lives. A few weeks later the village chief sent for him.

"O doctor of white men," said this chief,

"you have done what our own medicine men could not do. We are grateful for your help, given when death kept counsel here. But you do not want us to pay you with our horses, or our women, so we pay you in paleface gold."

Whereupon they blindfolded him, put him on a horse, and rode with him for about three hours. Then they removed the blindfold.

There in front of the doctor was the richest outcropping of ore he had ever heard of, many nuggets worth small fortunes in themselves. The doctor filled two saddle bags with them, was again blindfolded and carried back to the village. With this generous pay for his professional services he retired to live a life of luxury and ease.

"Old Tom," another Indian well known among whites, used to insist that strange and eerie supernatural beings lived in Supersitition Mountain. He said that the Thunder Gods and the Gods of Greed held council every third moon among the crags and pinnacles there.

Probably he was right. He was a wise old man, wise enough to know that the greatest treasures are intangible, certainly are seldom found in the form of yellow metal.

12. Maps of the Lost Mine

UNDOUBTEDLY the Paralta family and later Jacob Walz had maps that showed the location of the gold store in Superstition. If you knew precisely how to get one of these maps, and how to follow it after you got it, you might have a fortune at hand. Adolf Ruth sensed that fortune, and whoever murdered him and stole his map may have profited thereby.

If you just spread the word around a bit in Arizona, some loyal citizen will pop up pretty soon and offer to sell you a map, with a corking story thrown in. A man in El Paso, Texas, once paid $500 for a map of the Lost Dutchman Mine, but it was stolen from him. L. C. Fellows of St. Louis paid $50 for such a map once, got cold feet and sold it the same day for $100. He doesn't know what the buyer did with it.

George Holmes, son of Dick Holmes, who saw the Dutchman die, has been in Superstition Mountain many times, and one day a stranger came to him seeking information.

"Sure," George told him, "anybody can go and look for the mine. It belongs to whoever finds it, I reckon."

"You know the mountain pretty well?"

"Yes, I do."

"How about water, and trails, and all that, Mr. Holmes?"

"Well — yep — just give me a pencil and paper — here —"

Mr Holmes took a piece of wrapping paper from a parcel he carried, squatted on the sidewalk and began penciling. He sketched the mountain very roughly, showed Apache Trail, then Weaver's Needle and several more peaks. some of the main canyons.

Then he put a cross on the drawing and said to the man, "Now this here marks First Water Ranch, where you ought to make your base camp. It's easy to locate, and a safe place to start. Work out through the mountain from there, study your landmarks, and you ought to be all right. First Water is about eight miles from Weaver's Needle. But be careful."

The stranger thanked Mr. Holmes, took the crude drawing and went his way. Mr. Holmes saw no more of him.

Seven years later, in another part of the state, another stranger accosted Mr. Holmes.

"I hear tell," said this stranger, "that you are interested in the Lost Dutchman Mine."

"Well, some."

"Good! Now for $100 cash, Mr. Holmes, I'll sell you this map that shows you the location of it — see here, this cross mark shows the exact spot where the mine is at. You can't go wrong."

There was Mr. Holmes' map, come back to him!

Now, because human nature is what it is, and because some of you good readers will "have

80

an urge," I have consulted the sheriff of Maricopa County, Arizona, for you, asking him to give his most serious advice to men and women who would brave the dangers of Superstition Mountain. Here is what he said:

First, don't go. If you are a tenderfoot you'll be taking too many chances.

Second when you do decide to go (as you doubtless will anyway), don't worry about getting a map. Better make a map as you go into the mountain, carefully noting the landmarks and the trail you take so that you can get out again, else some other prospector a few years later will likely stumble onto your bleaching bones. It may be romantic and brave and adventurous to challenge the mountain alone, but it isn't sensibe. Many a man has found that out.

Choose the winter months to make your search. It seldom gets dangerously cold, but you have a far better chance of finding water in the mountain then. In summer the chances are about ten to one that you will die of thirst — if somebody doesn't murder you first.

If you can possibly do so, get three or four able-bodied men to go with you. In numbers there is strength. Carry good rifles and side arms.

Wear strong shoes with thick soles. Know what to do for snakebite, for sprained ankles, for thorn pricks. Know how to cook over an open fire without utensils. Know how to bed down under the velvety star-gemmed sky. Know what to do when a coyote screams crazily at you, and when you come unexpectedly onto a herd of wild javalinas.

Probably it will be foolish, now, to look for the stripped palo verde tree with the pointing arm, which was the Dutchman's key to his treasure. In the years since he died the tree must have died, too, else new growth would have changed it so that the pointing limb would be hard to identify. Nevertheless, it would do no harm to inspect all the older palo verdes with some care. You just might strike a hot clue!

The ironwood logs with which "Old Snow Beard" concealed his mine shaft ought to be about ready to cave in, but maybe not. Ironwood is almost literally wood that is iron. Pieces of it are known to lie on the open desert for centuries, defiant of rain and cold and sun, weathering a bit but remaining so heavy and hard that they will sink in water (ironwood is the second hardest wood known). Perhaps,

82

though, rain over the decades has washed some of the dirt and rocks off the logs, so as to reveal them, or perhaps to reveal a surface outcropping of the rich ore itself. Look alert!

Intelligent persons, unfamiliar with the West or with Superstition especially, naturally will say, "Well, how is it that the mine hasn't already been found again, if so many persons have been searching through the years? It would seem that the place has been gone over with a fine-tooth comb."

Not on your life!

Just make one trek in to Weaver's Needle, or even part way, and you will have answered your own question. No area in all North America is more savage. There lies a veritable maze of canyons, bewildering thousands of them, big and small. Mere man, there, becomes infinitesimal. Old flat, sprawling, eerie Superstition Mountain is good for centuries of mystery.

And yet — if her mood should so dictate — she might tomorrow reveal her incomparable riches. She has shown them before; doubtless she will again.

May you, therefore, be the next recipient of her ethereal favor.

The Author

OREN ARNOLD has produced hundreds of articles for major magazines and fifty-odd books, many with regional backgrounds. *Writer's Yearbook* has called him "the dean of western writers."

The reader may also be interested in two other new books by Oren Arnold: HIDDEN TREASURE IN THE WILD WEST, containing several of the best-loved legends of the region, and profusely illustrated; and IRONS IN THE FIRE, presenting the fascinating lore of cattle brands and branding, along with some lost-gold legends.